Sticky Murphy – Lover of Life

STICKY MURPHY
LOVER OF LIFE

SECOND WORLD WAR
CLANDESTINE
LYSANDER
AND INTRUDER
MOSQUITO
PILOT WING COMMANDER
ALAN MICHAEL
'STICKY' MURPHY
DSO AND BAR, DFC,
CROIX DE GUERRE

BY JAMES H. COLEY

Published in 2018 by Fighting High Ltd,
www.fightinghigh.com

British Library Cataloguing-in-Publication data.
A CIP record for this title is available from the
British Library.

ISBN – 13: 978-1-9998128-4-3

Designed and typeset in Adobe Minion 11/15pt
by Michael Lindley and Alice Kendall.
www.truthstudio.co.uk.

Printed and bound by Gomer Press.
Front cover design by www.truthstudio.co.uk.

*The Greeks said a man is immortal as long as his name
is remembered on earth*

Contents

Foreword

By Peter James Coley

Peter James Coley

My father, and author, James H. Coley (Jim) was a flight sergeant in No. 23 Squadron during the Second World War, under the command of clandestine and intruder pilot, Wing Commander Alan Michael Murphy (known as 'Sticky') DSO & Bar, DFC, Croix de Guerre.

'Sticky' was an absolute inspiration to his squadron both on and off duty and my father was consequently motivated and inspired to write a book dedicated to his memory and honour, many years after the war. The book consisted of Part 1 and Part 2 which Jim typed himself, carrying out extremely wide and careful research and combining his memories, and those of others who had served in No. 23 Squadron.

My father died on 24 February 1992. At his funeral some No. 23 Squadron surviving airmen were in attendance as he was lowered into his grave at Wimborne Cemetery in Dorset, while an RAF bugler played 'The Last Post'. As his son I decided at his funeral that Part 1 and Part 2 of his book would be best handed to No. 23 Squadron. At the time I was on auto pilot and handed over the 'Sticky Murphy' book without retaining a copy. However I managed to locate a copy of Part 2 after some years but unfortunately was unable, despite considerable effort over 20 years and worldwide search, to find Part 1 of the book.

Out of passion for what No. 23 Squadron had achieved during the war and with a sense of duty to my father, I was about to publish just Part 2 on its own when unbelievably Part 1 turned-up hidden away in the loft of our house.

Thanks go to Tommy Cushing, for providing photos and information. Tommy was a young boy living near 'Little Snoring' aerodrome in Norfolk when No. 23 Squadron were stationed there in 1944, and who consequently met the airmen after they had served in Malta GC and Italy on clandestine and intruder sorties. Thanks also go to Gail, Sticky's daughter who lives in South Africa, for her assistance, and to Pete Smith, who I received contact details for from No. 23 Squadron Buddy Badley's widow.

It was said that those who knew 'Sticky' (Lover of Life) can still hear his infectious laugh and recall his joy of living and indomitable personality. The final words are quoted from his citation for the award of the Bar to his Distinguished Service Order. 'This officer has participated in a large number of sorties, involving a wide range of targets. His outstanding skill, gallant leadership and iron determination have been reflected in the fine fighting qualities of his squadron which has won much success.' Let there be no doubt that in any Valhalla of warriors, Sticky Murphy can sit beside his contemporaries like Guy Gibson, VC, DSO, DFC, on equal terms and with a smile.

Publisher's note
This book was originally written in the 1970s and 1980s and Jim Coley passed away in 1992. As such the reader should note that some references to addresses may not be current. In addition, one page of the original manuscript remains lost. We felt this should not be a hindrance to publishing such an important book. The location of this missing page is indicated in the book.

James H. Coley. *(Peter Coley)*

Authors Note

Wing Commander Murphy's widow, sister and daughter asked why this book was researched and written more than thirty and forty years after his death on 2 December 1944. 'So that his only child, grandchildren and descendants (as well as his contemporaries) should know the qualities of a man who lived life to the fullest, and appeared to love every minute of it', was the only answer.

On his arrival in Malta in late September 1943, when we first met, Squadron Leader Murphy had carried out thirty-six operational sorties against the enemy, many being unusually hazardous and daring.

I recall a night in January 1944, sitting exhausted and depressed in a meal tent in Alghero, Sardinia. He was at the other end of the table, also with head in hands. He looked up, surprised to find a companion. We exchanged smiles, without words. News of my expected baby was overdue. He, too, had a child coming. Nature had a habit of preparing to replace losses in perilous operational careers – in advance.

This biography may be the outcome of that incident. Murphy was an enigma to us, with the contrast of his Englishness, yet Irish name and wildness.

It is not contended that a good deal of persons referred to in this book suffered anything like the hardships of others, or were more brave or intrepid than many, apart from Colonel Jean Cassart and 'Wings' Day. Sticky Murphy would have been the first to decry any other contention – so long as praise was given to his squadrons – yet his name, even after thirty or forty years, still evokes a smile – often a laugh – with an uplift of hearts of those who knew him.

At John Nesbitt-Dufort's funeral in 1975, a loud and spontaneous laugh came from someone whose memory of Sticky ended in 1942. The old comrade said: 'Oh! Sticky Murphy. He was a splendid chap!' Whether ex-Serviceman or civilian, mention of Sticky's name brought a similar response.

My pilot in those days – Bill Shattock – has continued to be a close friend for well over forty years, and thanks are recorded for his encouragement and help. Well-known writer Miles Tripp, a former operational airman, was the first to offer guidance and assistance, as did Wing Commander Norman Conquer, OBE (a veteran of Malta, Italy and Sardinia). Other old comrades helped readily, including David Atherton, John Irvin, George Twitt and Jock Reid, Sticky's navigator for many trips. Wing Commanders John Nesbitt-Dufort, DSO, Croix de Guerre, and Philip Russell, DFC, respectively Sticky's close friend in 1941/42, and successor as commanding officer of No. 23 Squadron, were also keen supporters. To these I must add Buddy Badley (still flying Jumbos into 1978), Bill Gregory, Tommy Cushing (enthusiastic historian of Little Snoring), Air Chief Marshal Sir Lewis Hodges, KCB, CBE, DSO (foremost in Special Operations) and Colonel Jean Cassart of the Belgian Army – whose destiny was linked with Sticky Murphy's in 1941.

Above all, grateful thanks are given to Wing Commander Murphy's family, including his widow, sister, daughter and cousin, who gave unstinted help with research material and recollections.

Final acknowledgements are appreciatively recorded to Edith Heed, without whose patient and efficient secretarial assistance and cheerful encouragement, the task would have failed long ago.

A eulogy was not the aim or intention, but the Cromwellian doctrine of 'warts and all'. This is how the man was, according to many who knew him. The chapter entitled 'Tributes' shows the wide spectrum of his admirers. Contemporary diaries, photographs and flying logbooks, with almost total recall by many, contributed to his story. If he had a flaw it would have emerged.

Grieve not for Sticky Murphy and the others – they live on in memories and in children and grandchildren. In the case of Shorty Dawson's navigator – Fergie Murray – one of my sons carries his name. Murray's crew left an imprint on history in the Shell House Gestapo headquarters raid in March 1945 at Copenhagen. They were lost, but come still in my dreams.

The world of old comrades, now grandfathers galore, must be those of the gladiators of Rome – morituri te salutamus (We who are about to die salute you). Soon no man will survive to tell his story, and history is notoriously academic.

23 November 1986
Kingsbridge, South Devon

Chapter One

Arrival Malta – September 1943

Four sunburnt men stood apart – lean and hungry. They wore khaki shirts and slacks, Mae Wests and carried parachutes. The white runway of Maltese stone, and barren landscape, contrasted with the blue sky of a hot September day in 1943. From the surrounding Mediterranean came a slight breeze.

One man, already a legend – a short, bronzed Australian flight sergeant pilot – shaded his eyes to reinforce a wide-brimmed bush hat. He was Shorty Dawson, a character full of strange oaths. Frequently teased as coming from Woolamaloo or Wagga Wagga, Shorty in fact hailed from Ballera. All eyes focused on the sparkling object descending sharply towards the runway.

'What sort of Pommy bastards will these be, Ferg?' murmured Shorty to his English navigator, Fergie Murray. 'Might even be Aussies with some luck.'

Fergie snorted, 'Wait and see. Let's hope he doesn't hit the edge of the bloody wadi and write it off before he gets here.'

The men watched with idle interest. The ache of exile was on them all. Even to Shorty this contact always aroused mixed emotions. Yesterday two strangers had set course from Cornwall. They brought recent papers and news of bombing from home. Here, was Luqa Aerodrome, Malta GC. Reinforcements were arriving for the depleted squadron.

A steep glide approach at 140 knots, perfect landing, and the glistening new Mk VI Mosquito taxied to the battered dispersal hut. The reception committee, now joined by several 'erks', watched curiously.

Harshly the two Rolls-Royce Merlin engines cleared their throats, the aircraft door slowly opened, and two figures clambered down the ladder. The pilot appeared second, tall and slim, in a black one-piece flying suit. He removed his flying helmet and shook his head. A pale face emerged, decorated with a curly RAF-type moustache. About six feet tall, he had a tousled head of light brown hair, protruding ears and chiselled features. With a frank gaze he surveyed the scene as he stroked his moustache, upswept on both 'wings'. The physique and movements of an athlete completed his appearance.

Shorty ducked under the starboard airscrew. 'You've got a right good oil leak there mate. Starboard motor!'

'Really old boy, many thanks,' replied the pilot, grinning boyishly to reveal regular white teeth. 'My name is Murphy. Where's the bog?'

Shorty's hackles bristled – this strange Pom was beating him at his own game. His accent was too English for the Aussie's ears. 'We don't bother much with them here, mate. Try the back of the hut. Might be a bucket there.'

They exchanged a few more words. The stranger stripped off his Mae West and overalls and saying 'Thanks', strode off to the rear of the nearby hut.

Shorty wandered over to the other airmen. They were curious. 'Well, Shortstuff?' said another navigator, Jim, with an enquiring lift of the eyebrows.

'A Pommy squadron leader named Murphy with a row of gongs. Must be the new flight commander. I was hoping it might be Charlie Scherf. Calls himself 'Stinky' or somethin'. He's a saucy bastard. We're going to have trouble with that joker. He's been around.'

This was a major speech from the normally laconic Australian. Only the size of 'Pommy Sheilas' (as he called English girls) usually impressed Shorty. Repeatedly he was told, 'From where you stand they all look big!'

The two crews walked to their Mosquitoes for flight testing on the way to an advanced landing strip in Sicily. His companions pondered on the new arrivals and Dawson's hostile reaction to the pilot. The sight of decorated squadron leaders was nothing new, but NCO aircrews suspected trouble. They had enough of that.

'The bastard told me they fly OK on one engine,' said Shorty. Within the past few days he and Fergie had passed an agonising three hours on one engine. Flying through moonlit mountain valleys, nursing the aircraft from 200 feet over a target at Foggia to a maximum of 4,000 feet to reach Sicily, they landed at Palermo by the lights of two Jeeps. 'I told him not to count on it out here, because of the temps,' Shorty added. Overheating Merlin engines were a problem.

This shed more light on the newcomer. The other crew had suffered a similar crippled flight within the last week before making a lucky forced landing at night in no man's land when the other engine failed. Posted 'Missing in Action' they knew how fortunate they had been to survive.

'He'll find out', was their opinion.

'Think I'll call the toffee-nosed sod "Whiskers" Murphy,' remarked Shorty as they parted company.

The two Mosquitoes skimmed sea and land in close formation at low level to land on the mud of the Plain of Catania. There they refuelled. In the early hours of the next day both crews took off to intrude on and bomb aerodromes near Rome.

In late September 1943 the elite Mosquito intruder squadron – No. 23 of the Royal Air Force – was ending nine months' service in Malta. Seconded from Fighter Command primarily to attack the night bombers of Malta at their bases, tactical support of armies in the field became an additional function. Night bombing and strafing of Rommel's retreating Afrika Corps in Libya and Tunisia complemented the daylight attacks of the Desert Air Force, giving the Axis troops a foretaste of the vengeance to come in Europe.

The 'soft underbelly of Europe', as Winston Churchill chose to describe Sicily and Italy, now received the first Allied blows. At last air superiority began to tell. The Eighth and Fifth Armies of the Allies started their long slog, destined to be so costly in men and materiel.

'Just like galloping a racehorse on a ploughed field – bloody stupid' was the opinion of the other pilot, Bill Shattock, when it came to operating the thoroughbred de Havilland Mosquito from such mud bases. A farmer, he thought it sacrilegious to abuse such a mechanical aristocrat.

With four 20mm Hispano cannons, each firing 600 shells per minute, and four .303 machine guns, each firing 1,200 rounds per minute, the

Mosquito was a formidable instrument of war.

Weather conditions worsened in the central Mediterranean – vile by any standards that winter. Only eleven crews and six aircraft were available at one time – half of the crews and one-quarter of the aircraft establishment. Wastage by casualties and tour expiry, despite regular reinforcements, caused emergency measures to be taken to remain operational.

Conditions were improving as Squadron Leader Murphy arrived, but sensing low morale in 'B' Flight, which he had come to command, he acted. Within a few days he invaded the jealously guarded privacy of the NCOs at Balluta mess, Sliema. He walked into the room shared by Shorty and his mates, bearing four bottles of wine.

'I've been checking up. You chaps have been holding the fort,' he said, cheerfully ignoring the surprised looks. 'Let's have a drink. You can give me the gen.'

As some of the wine was drunk, a desultory conversation followed. Puzzled men probed his flying history. He was reticent – in contrast to his open manner. This increased suspicion, and both pilots and navigators were vague about tactics, weather conditions and targets. They were not to know of his earlier exploits more than a year before – still highly secret. All were likely to fall into enemy hands. Unspoken thoughts arose. Was he a phoney hero? One of those who spoke of sergeants' weather when black clouds were low? A day-fighter chappy who found the darkness disconcerting?

Later it was agreed that it was a pity if Murphy was some sort of glory seeker, as he seemed a decent type for the new flight commander replacing Paul Rabone. However, the first murky weather would show. The mountains, dodgy compasses and generally unfavourable flying conditions soon sorted everyone out.

They were to find that night flying was his métier. The worse the weather the more he revelled in it. He was the antithesis of the special weather types. If it was filthy he flew first on many occasions. If the runway was stupidly short, or bombs were to be carried off a runway of dubious surface, Sticky Murphy was the first airborne – day and night. 'If I get off OK, you chaps follow,' he joked. That was leadership.

His effervescent personality and joy of living was infectious. Morale improved almost at once. Sticky's panache and gregarious nature were apparent. Messes often rang with his solo rendering of 'Rip my knickers away' in a robust, but discordant, attacking style. The squadron song followed, proclaiming the lads to be a 'shower of bastards who preferred fornication to fighting'. One wit, who affected to dislike obscenities, paraphrased the words to 'I'd sooner chase women than Focke Wulfs!' No party – and there were many – was in full flight until Sticky had let rip. Many more would have been held, but when bats were walking because of the weather, he was leading the way into the air – ever the foremost.

'Always have a go!' was Sticky's attitude, and Semper Aggressus, the official squadron motto, best translated in that way. It could have been made for him, so close was he to Admiral Lord Horatio Nelson's dictum of offensive war. Sticky's own motto was another translation, echoing the ANZAC war cry at Gallipoli – 'Right lads – after the bastards!'

But what had fashioned such an extraordinary man, without class consciousness or bombast and with a love of life that made every moment an exciting and happy challenge? All this was spontaneous without apparent effort or motive.

Chapter Two

Ancestry and Childhood

What makes a man? This has long been a talking point. Is heredity or environment the main factor in development of character and personality?

Alan Michael Murphy was born on 26 September 1917 (the same month and year as Group Captain Leonard Cheshire, VC) at Cockermouth in the Lake District. This was close to the Irish Sea, over which Alan's great-great-grandfather had come from Ulster generations before. The name Murphy and the Protestant religion were an unusual combination, and Alan's father Isaac, known as George, shipowner and broker, was born nearby at Whitehaven on 20 January 1872.

Alan's mother, born Ethel Moore at Morland, Westmorland, lost her father at the age of five. Her mother brought up a young family with the courage that was a feature of women bereaved before, during and after the First World War. George and Ethel married in 1906.

Captain Thomas Murphy, Alan's great-grandfather, drowned in Dublin's River Liffey, when swimming for help from an upturned boat. Those who clung to the boat were rescued. Family legend speaks of another ancestor being in the area during the Indian Mutiny involving the Black Hole of Calcutta in 1756, while Jack Balmer, Ethel's uncle, was in Africa with Cecil Rhodes, empire builder.

Chest trouble made George unable to follow familial sea tradition, and his family spent 1923–28 in Johannesburg, South Africa. The climate greatly improved his condition and laid a foundation for Alan's physique and personality. It was there that young Alan Murphy quickly showed his independence and fighting spirit. When his sister intervened in a fight against uneven odds, by riding a bicycle into the fray, she was told that he would prefer to fight his own battles in future.

Early in 1974 this author stood at the modest terraced house where Alan Murphy was born – 'Rydal Mere', Fitz Road, Cockermouth. It was interesting to hear one of the inhabitants say, 'The elite lived here in 1917', as he confirmed Murphy's birthplace. Another octogenarian, speaking of George Murphy, said: 'He was not here long, but I remember him as a fine, tall, upstanding gentleman.'

Cockermouth drowsed in the spring sunshine, and 'Rydal Mere' continued to overlook the river, linen mill and narrow contemporary world. The nearby sea ports of Maryport and Workington struggled on, where once thrived shipping and iron trades.

Alan's elder sister, Mrs Doreen Gravestock of Barton Seagrave near Kettering, recalled their close and happy relationship throughout his life. From the earliest days she remembered him as an impulsive child, full of energy and enthusiasm, with a cheerful, laughing, very popular personality. Even at a young age his charm was evident.

Their father George was a fine man of somewhat Victorian attitude, loved and respected by his wife and children. After South Africa had boosted his health, he reached the age of eighty-four. With a dry sense of humour, George liked a drink and a party, and encouraged his children in all games and sports, finding pride in their achievements. He taught both offspring to swim in South Africa. Alan's only child, Gail, and her husband and two children, now live near Johannesburg. Ethel Murphy told her progeny that, as a girl, she could run faster and jump higher than her contemporaries. Alan inherited this ability to the full and his competitive spirit and determination made him a formidable opponent. When the family returned from South Africa, Alan attended Seafield Preparatory School at Lytham near Blackpool, from 1928 to 1931. The headmaster was a friend of his father. The school describes Alan at the age of twelve as 'A very energetic centre half. Full of dash and determination and a tower of strength.'

At Seafield he had a close friend named Alan Chalmers. In order to differentiate between the two boys, Mrs Chalmers called Alan Murphy 'Sticky', having misunderstood her son's suggestion of a nickname. From the age of nineteen he used this sobriquet in family correspondence and otherwise for the rest of his life.

By 1929 the Murphy family had found a home adjoining the Dormy Hotel, beside Ferndown Golf Club in the New Forest. The house called 'Morland' now forms part of the hotel, overlooking the Ferndown road to Bournemouth. Doreen Gravestock recollects:

Due to the constant moving before the family settled at Ferndown in 1929, we found little opportunity to make lasting friends, so that Sticky and I formed a great friendship which lasted throughout his life. We were both keen on games and swam, sailed, played tennis, golf and squash together. Our father, George, was a very keen sportsman and always expected us to do well at games. He never said very much but he was really very proud of Sticky. I think his only disappointment was when Sticky said he wanted to join the Royal Air Force instead of going to sea, but he did not try to change his mind in any way.

I remember when Sticky was at his prep school at Lytham, George was asked to play cricket in the parents' match. Sticky said: 'Now don't make a duck will you?'

George was one of the 'do or die' brigade of batsmen and he survived just three balls. He scored 6–6–4 and was out. I am sure he did not make the highest score for the parents, but it was certainly the most entertaining innings.

From 1931 until 1936 Alan attended Canford School, long established near Wimborne in the tranquil county of Dorset. A fine public school with sporting traditions, noted for character buildings and situated a few miles from the family home at Ferndown, Canford was an ideal place for the young Murphy to develop in all directions at once – which was his style. Regularly he arrived home without warning, bringing a horde of hungry friends. Ethel Murphy showed her gentle capabilities, catering for and welcoming warmly whoever arrived, and in whatever muddy or famished state. A secure and loving home was undoubtedly the foundation of Alan Murphy's life and personality.

Of surviving masters of those days, one, Yvone Kirkpatrick, OBE, TD – a former First World War fighter pilot on Sopwith Camels in the

Royal Flying Corps – remembered in 1974 that Alan Murphy was a born leader, and an athlete with a cheerful smile and tremendous determination. By coincidence, Kirkpatrick's commanding officer on No. 203 Squadron long ago was the officer who re-formed No. 23 Squadron of the Royal Air Force in 1925. Later, Air Vice Marshal Raymond Collishaw, CB, DSO, OBE, DSC, DFC, prominent among the air aces of the First World War, was an outstanding commander in the Middle East during 1940–41. Alan Murphy's destiny was inexorably linked with the same No. 23 Squadron. It was enlightening in 1974 to hear the clear recollection of Mr Kirkpatrick at his home, where we were joined by Alan's former housemaster, Robin Graham of Exeter, a forthright clear-thinking schoolmaster. The family considered him to have been a major influence on young Murphy. Mr Graham recalled what a cheerful, valuable, active and useful member of his house Alan Murphy had been, with his chief characteristic that he was completely fearless at all games, but remained modest.

At Canford our subject became an under officer in the Officers' Training Corps, which involved numerous exercises requiring organisation and discipline. He also served as a chapel monitor at Canford Magna Church within the school grounds, and spent long periods there, his name now appearing on the Roll of Honour.

Schooldays in Dorset developed Alan Murphy's character, personality and physique. He jumped high and long, as well as being a hurdler and quarter-miler. Gradually he matured and studied hard to achieve entry as a flight cadet at Royal Air Force Cranwell.

In 1975, Mr Stewart Strain of New Milton in the New Forest, senior classical master from 1930 to 1953 at Canford School, was pleased to recall Alan Murphy's particular qualities in his last years through a unique sideline society named the Canford Outcasts Cricket Club. Special traits required for election involved unselfishness, bonhomie and similar attributes – natural virtues that Murphy possessed, together with a classic outlook for which public schools were not noted. Cricket matches in the traditional village style – light-hearted and boozy, with much bread, cheese and beer, and (in Dorset style) singing together – were the object of the club.

Alan Murphy was not a great cricketer, but shone by his easy, genial personality. He was much better at rugby, but in 1936 was duly appointed 'Chief Club Entertainer', which meant that even if it was not his turn to play in the team, he went along to help in the way of social enjoyment, which was to leave happy memories for so many, and cemented local connections.

Mr Strain also recalled how at the Christmas dinner of an Outcasts' reunion for past and present members, Alan Murphy behaved with impeccable good humour and fine manners, after a fair amount of beer. Those days may well have been the foundation of a remarkable ability on Murphy's part to handle substantial quantities of liquor with great humour, and remarkable sobriety, to which many Royal Air Force comrades, including this author, willingly attest. The comment was made about his raucous singing style, only compensated for, some conceded, by the unusual vigour and actions so appreciated in a Service mess.

Another side of his personality emerged in the recollection of Rear Admiral Rodney Sturdee, CB, DSC, a younger contemporary at Canford. In 1974 the admiral remembered Murphy as the prototype of the 'beloved leader' who was dormitory prefect and who, on at least one occasion, fell asleep while kneeling in prayer beside his bed. Perhaps this demonstrated his genuine piety and the energy that he expended each day. Meeting him at one of the aforesaid Christmas dinners of the Outcasts showed that he had begun to develop his panache, and certainly his love of life and ability to live it to the full.

To add to the names by which Alan Michael Murphy was known during his life, there is a version by his cousin, Pat Murphy, a few years his senior, who knew him as 'Mick'. Pat, a cheerful character with an open personality that he shared with Mick, his sister Doreen and Mick's daughter Gail, was the son of Alan Murphy's uncle on his father's side. Now living in Yorkshire he remembered 'Mick's' return from South Africa when they went on beach picnics together. One visit was noteworthy for the daring exploits of the young Alan, who defied gravity on overhanging rocks. Later, on a picnic to Lulworth Cove with Ethel Murphy, when her son had attended Canford School, a more significant event occurred. From time to time, as they swam and sunbathed, there appeared overhead an extraordinary, rickety biplane, which seemed in imminent danger of crashing into the sea. This fascinated the young Mick Murphy, who bubbled over with excitement, and wished to take a trip in it, which was believed to be available from a nearby field. Pat Murphy viewed this proposition with some misgivings, but the party made the journey to the field, only to find that flights had ceased for the day. While Pat was relieved, Mick was disappointed, but in view of later events, Pat wondered if it was this incident that had led Mick away from the seafaring tradition of the family.

At Canford, in addition to sport, Alan Murphy persisted in his studies of English, History, French, Mathematics, Physics, Geography, Divinity, Latin and Chemistry. There was a rigorous persistence by schoolmasters to avoid youthful students neglecting studies in favour of the plethora of sporting activities open to them. Murphy realised that the ambition he had now formed to fly required hard study and he pressed on, with some cramming in French to supplement regular lessons.

Murphy was successful in 1935 in passing with Credit (equivalent to the modern GCSE) in the first six subjects listed above in the Oxford University Local Examinations – commonly called the Oxford School Certificate. This enabled him to sit exams and attend selection procedures that gained him entry to the Royal Air Force at Cranwell as a flight cadet, an achievement shared with few of his fellows from the many applicants.

Now was the opportunity that challenged him, and his colleagues, to qualify for air pilots and leaders, with fast-growing technology and horizons of attainment only glimpsed at the beginning.

Chapter Three

Pilot Training at RAF College, Cranwell

Upon arrival at the Royal Air Force College, Cranwell, on the flatness of Lincolnshire, Alan Murphy met his old prep school chum Alan Chalmers, to be greeted by his old nickname of 'Sticky', which stayed with him. They were delighted to renew their friendship.

His first unit was with 'B' Squadron in September 1936. Strict discipline, necessary to fashion adolescents into fighting airmen, was a change from the atmosphere at school. Fierce personal and Service pride now became the order of the day. Competition was great, and any faltering or half-hearted characters quickly departed. Instructors were the cream of the Service, and set examples by which cadets would mould their future deportment and leadership. Traditions ruled. Less than 100 cadetships were awarded each year. Excellence was the only standard.

Quickly, Sticky Murphy – just nineteen – grew to manhood, maturing and developing his flair for spontaneous and lasting friendships. His happy and uninhibited personality made most ordinary happenings events to remember. He had found his true element, and life was great.

One of the few survivors of his close friends at Cranwell is Group Captain Brian Kingcome, DSO, DFC, a fighter pilot of distinction in the Battle of Britain and thereafter. Now a modest businessman with a young family, he has said:

Sticky and I were on the same course at Cranwell. We were two of a fivesome of cadets who became close friends during the two years we were there, spending most of our off-duty hours together during both term time and leaves. Sadly I was the only one to survive.

After all these years I remember him clearly and all the great qualities that made him so memorable a companion. But most of all there stays in my mind his zest and enthusiasm for life, the respect and affection he inspired in all who knew him, and his gaiety and panache that masked an iron will.

While the epitome of the disciplined pilot, devoted to the traditions of the Royal Air Force, Sticky's puckish sense of humour remained. His words are on record, showing his tongue often in cheek. Two forced landings when his engine conked out during aerobatics produced the note: 'Fan stopped – landed successfully.'

Another time, it is said he was invited to take tea with the commandant's daughter. Sticky arrived 'on the dot' by crashing an aircraft almost in her lap. His note on the photograph of the pranged machine says: ''Oo done it? It was a sudden gust of wind, and I'm sticking to that story.'

Pat Murphy remembers:

Mick and I met [up] when he was a cadet at Cranwell. I was in Lincolnshire on business and called at Cranwell to meet him. We went into Grantham for a meal, visited a couple of pubs and returned to the college where he introduced me to some fellow cadets and showed me various things of interest.

It was apparent to me that Mick was absorbed with anything to do with flying and almost persuaded me to join the RAF forthwith.

Around about 1937/38 Mick's father suddenly decided that it would be a splendid thing for himself, and other members of the family, to make a pilgrimage from time to time, for the benefit of our health, to a hydro and there to take the waters. Mick and I were included in the party.

Smedleys Hydro at Matlock was decided upon. This was an excellent establishment, with first-class food, Turkish baths, dancing and anything likely to make for a happy life, except for one thing – no bar! It was strictly a temperance hotel, and any suggestion of alcoholic refreshment was deeply frowned upon by the management.

However, this did not present any great obstacle as there was a pub

on the opposite side of the road, and this became a welcome
rendezvous before meals and so forth.

The question of smuggling in bottles of gin was relatively simple;
excellent parties were held in our rooms. The empties disappeared
through the window into the bushes below.

However, it did seem to a number of the more sober guests that the
waters of the hydro excited a more stimulating effect on some more
than others.

Wing Commander J.E.T. Haile recalled in 1977:

I did not see Sticky after 1938 but my memory of him was of a long-
limbed, happy person, not easily thrown off balance, and one who
possessed a good deal of hidden 'steel' in his make-up. Our instructors
at Cranwell in all subjects and at all levels were of high standing.
During 1937 we had a visit from the Top Brass of the re-born German
Air Force (Milch, Stumpff and Udet). All flying was halted until the
Germans had landed, and, of course, there was no VHF radio control.
The result was that a large gaggle of Avro Tutors, Hart Trainers,
Audaxes and Furies were waiting to take off, flown by instructors and
pupils at all stages in the art. As luck would have it the wind was
blowing diagonally towards the hangars, so that take-off was across
rather than down the main landing area.

When a green Very light from the Watch Office gave the OK to get
airborne, the sky was suddenly full of aircraft taking straight off from
in front of their own hangars, and all climbing away at different
speeds and heights, with some turning before the others – like a covey
of birds disturbed – a positively dangerous sight. Milch turned to
Dermot Boyle (our chief flying instructor) and said: 'Ach! I see you
have no circuit rules!' Fortunately Udet (the air ace) spoke up and
said: 'Ah, but it teaches them to keep their eyes open.' I like to think
these were prophetic words and that Sticky was a magnificent product
of that training environment.

The very name Murphy was incompatible with his Englishness of speech
and manner. His personality showed unique spontaneity and zest.

Records show that he boxed at the college – winning of course.

Murphy's first flight in a Royal Air Force aircraft began at 14.24 hours on 17 September 1936 in an Avro Tutor biplane, with Flight Lieutenant Morgan-Smith as his instructor. The regulation sequences of tuition consisted of taxiing, take-offs, straight and level flying, stalling, climbing, gliding, turning, approaches, landings, preliminary action in the event of fire, starting, stopping engines and spinning. Sticky flew solo in the Tutor on 13 October that year. Then followed the graded forms of instruction, including night flying – a foretaste of his destined operational life.

In April 1937 Murphy flew the more advanced Hawker Hart and Audax, gaining experience, albeit with two crashes. On 30 July Sticky received an official assessment at Cranwell – 'Possesses dash and courage.'

Flight Cadet Murphy now became an under officer, leader of his flight, and captain of the college athletics team. In the annual triangular match between officer cadets of the Royal Military College, Sandhurst, the Royal Military Academy, Woolwich, and the Royal Air Force College, Cranwell, he shone repeatedly, improving the long-jump record of the RAF in 1938 to twenty-three feet and one and three-quarter inches, which stood for many years.

Cranwell College Journal recalled in the autumn of 1938 that captain of athletics, Alan Murphy, was suffering with a stye on one eye. It was the day of the athletics match against the Milocarians, and he was allowed to watch the event on condition that he did not participate. Seeing that things were not going well for the college captain, Murphy quickly changed, won the long jump, and ran in the hurdles under the nose of the nursing sister in charge of his ward. Despite his efforts, Cranwell College lost, on the last event, by two points. Thanks were registered to Alan Murphy for his example and energy in training, and his skill and success in the long jump, high jump and hurdles, which set a lead the team profoundly followed. Three times that season he had broken the RAF long-jump record.

Tuition and exercises – flying solo and in formation, performing aerobatics, cross-country navigation, practising emergency landings with simulated engine failure etc. – comprised much of the practical side of his instruction at Cranwell. First, and continuing, came the theoretical classwork. The theory of flight, navigation, armament, meteorology, instrumentation, signalling, engineering and geography, were directly connected with the flying aspect of his training.

The air as his element of operations meant that all components must be studied, as a mariner must know the sea. An airman also had to be a student of war on the land and at sea. Frequent need for inter-Service cooperation, and command of other forces later in a career, made this imperative.

Before 1939, much responsibility rested on the RAF for control and supervision of such tribal areas as the North West Frontier of India. The efficiency of the Service in this respect is well chronicled by the Marshal of the Royal Air Force Sir John Slessor, and Air Chief Marshal Sir Basil Embry. The by-product of such operations in Arab and Indian territories was a reservoir of flying and maintenance experience, which proved invaluable in the years that followed.

All officers in the General Duties branch of the RAF (the generic term for those on aircrew duties) also had to be capable of legal, ceremonial and disciplinary undertakings. It was from this branch that the most senior ranks were appointed. Temperament, nerve, integrity – all had to be tested repeatedly.

It chafed Sticky's adventurous spirit to study the Manual of Air Force Law, and similar publications. The Manual of Airmanship was meat and drink to him, because of the practical application. Nevertheless, he accepted the need for more academic studies as part of the complete professional attainment for which he aimed.

On 29 July 1938, Alan Michael Murphy qualified for the coveted 'Wings' and was awarded the King's Commission. Now he was a pilot officer – denoted by the thinnest of stripes on his sleeve. His career had begun, and he looked forward to the future, with an eager and confident air.

Chapter Four

RAF Service before Full Operational Career

Pilot Officer Murphy's first posting was to No. 185 Bomber Squadron, then equipped with Fairey Battle bombers. Powered by Rolls-Royce Merlin engines, they operated from Abingdon, south of Oxford.

In late August 1938, Sticky Murphy took his initial step to improve his skill in navigation, and enrolled in the Second-Class Navigators' Course at Manston on the Isle of Thanet, so close to Europe. Interesting exercises such as interception of surface craft (usually cross-Channel steamers), with a return to another base, improved professional competence. The testing of dead (deduced) reckoning navigation over the sea, and the calculation of the radius of action, brought confidence.

Close at hand was the 'drinkopolis' of Margate, Cliftonville and district. Many merry nights were spent at the height of the holiday season; high spirits brought release from discipline. Young men needed to recharge batteries and expend energies. Sticky continued his athletic training, and followed other pursuits including hill climbing in a small but lively car.

His agile build, warm personality and love of life made him a popular escort for young women. Inevitably, his family thought that each romance might be the one to last. Perhaps they did not appreciate his complete dedication to his profession at that time – and throughout his life. Certainly, before 1939, marriage was out of the question for a 'sprog' pilot officer.

Depleted and emasculated by successive Governments of both hues, the armed forces of the Crown struggled to fulfil their destiny, with maximum efficiency and minimum support. Commanders were more far-seeing than politicians.

Private companies and individuals combined in patriotic endeavour, aware of the emergency. German friendships and peace pledge movements developed, but the people's instincts were sound. As usual they were in advance of their political servants, who, as always, thought themselves the masters.

These were the days when the British aircraft industry of Blackburn, Bristol, Fairey Aviation, Handley Page, de Havilland, Hawker, A.V. Roe and Supermarine, fought for survival and development. The constant effort to design and build new types of aircraft exhausted many individuals. Urgency bred frustration as both main political parties kept their blinkers on, and resisted any sort of expenditure – mocking the voice of the 'enfant terrible', Winston Churchill, then labelled a 'warmonger'.

Sport and action filled off-duty life for Sticky Murphy and his comrades, and his quota of friendships remained full and lasting. In the meantime, the Ferndown family home, 'Morland', beckoned, with sea, sun and a happy family atmosphere. Friends of both sexes, cars just worthy of the name, and a jam-packed life consumed the present. Sticky's grandmother bought him his first jalopy, which expanded his range of operations.

Then it was back to No. 185 Squadron at Thornaby on Guy Fawkes' Day in 1938. The Munich Crisis of that year, and Chamberlain's piece of white paper, meant that Service chiefs at all levels could press on, relying upon efficiency and spirit to compensate for restricted financial budgets.

Sticky's cousin Pat Murphy recalls:

When Mick was a pilot officer at Thornaby I used to visit the northeast on business, and would let him know that I hoped to stay at the Metropole Hotel, Stockton-on-Tees on a certain date.

The appointed day would arrive and I would go into the bar at the Metropole about 6pm, order a quick half of beer, read the evening paper and await events in a quiet atmosphere.

The calm was shattered by Mick leading six to ten characters who roared into the pub. The first time this happened I really did wonder if they were the riot squad and if revolution had begun. The apprehensive looks of the barman and customers quickly

changed as the 'joie de vivre' of the invading customers set the scene
for one of jollity and great humour. Large quantities of ale were
consumed with dedicated fervour.

Usually after a somewhat hilarious session, I would be invited back
to the mess, where the party would continue till a late hour.

On one occasion, however, it was a Guest Night and Mick and the
boys were under an obligation to attend Mess Dinner and I could not
be invited. Unfortunately, while everyone had the best intention in the
world of attending the mess at the appointed hour, a game of Cardinal
Puff somehow sprang to life in the Metropole bar.

I was never really acquainted with the full facts of the case, but at a
later meeting I gathered that all was not well at the particular Guest
Night and a number of chairs were vacant owing to the dedication of
certain Cardinals and Popes who had been ordained at the Temple of
Metropole.

One meeting which does stand out in my memory was the night
that the squadron was having a dance.

The boys arrived at the Metropole Hotel for just a quick drink and
said that they had to return for this dance.

The only way I could attend was in evening dress. Obviously I did
not have evening dress with me so everyone got together and I was
transported back to their quarters where I was assured that within no
time at all I would be fixed up with the necessary outfit. Sure enough,
after a great deal of effort and the cooperation of all the officers on the
squadron, I was finally equipped with 'tails' – sleeves too short,
trousers too long, and a white shirt and bow tie under which I could
have ducked my head. I was then presented to the CO and his wife,
who stared with horrified incomprehension at the grotesque figure
before them standing with alcoholic cheerfulness in their midst.

On reflection I would hardly feel that it did anything to encourage
promotion for any of the officers involved in the operation. However,
as the evening mellowed, I imagine all was forgiven.

I look back on those days with great nostalgia and as some of the
happiest parties I have ever been privileged to attend.

The chaps I remember most vividly as Mick's particular friends
were Sam Moxham, Oxley and Cakebread. There were many others

whose names I have forgotten, but never will I forget the good times
that were had, and the cordiality and friendship that they gave.

There was one other meeting that I recall. On a sports day at
Thornaby I remember the outstanding popularity of Mick with all
ranks. He had that happy 'je ne sais quoi' of getting on with everyone.
No inhibitions and a complete gift for loving life. I have met many
people in my time, but never anyone who created and exuded
cheerfulness to the same degree as Mick.

He was a tremendous character and to be his friend was luck
indeed.

On 20 May 1939, Pilot Officer Murphy took part in balloon bursting,
series aerobatics and the fly-past at the Empire Air Day display. He flew
a Tutor in the first demonstrations and the Miles Magister in the fly-past.
Early in June 1939 No. 185 Squadron were being equipped with the
Handley Page Hampden bomber and moved to Cottesmore near Oakham
in the tiny county of Rutland. Here he was serving as a pilot officer on
3 September when the Second World War began.

Sticky spent the next few months in constant instruction on a war
footing, polishing his skills and training his crew to maximum efficiency
for the anticipated action to come.

Elder sister Doreen Gravestock recalled:

At one time I was stationed at a place called Wiverton Hall, near
Nottingham, and attached to 402 Battery, 50th Northants Regiment
of the Royal Artillery. Oddly enough Sticky had met members of this
regiment when he was stationed at Cottesmore and was particularly
friendly with Dennis King, who was later to become his best man.
Dennis was also best man at my wedding.

Wiverton Hall was situated in a very high position with a meadow
sloping away from it fairly steeply. Several times we would look out of
the downstairs window and see an aircraft flying almost window high
with the pilot giving the 'thumbs up'. Sticky had arrived for lunch.

In February 1940 Murphy was posted to the School of Navigation, St
Athan in South Wales, to carry out a specialist navigation course. The

title was No. 3 War Specialist Course, and until late May, he and other pilots flew advanced navigation exercises in Avro Anson aircraft. These embraced astronomical navigation and a series of flights around the coast of Britain, including the Channel Islands, Scillies, Isle of Man, Lundy and elsewhere. A total of eighty-three hours and fifteen minutes were recorded in the role of navigator, which were to be some of the best spent hours of his flying life.

After St Athan, Sticky was posted to Lossiemouth in Scotland. The date was 10 June 1940, the height of the German blitzkrieg on France. Determined not to miss the action at such a vital time, he stopped off at No. 3 Group headquarters, and, as second pilot with Squadron Leader Moneypenny in a Wellington, bombed bridges over the River Somme. Light flak was the only resistance. This was his first operational sortie against the enemy, and he was there unofficially – in passing as it were!

The events at Lossiemouth are best related by Sticky's wife Jean Murphy (née Leggat), who remembered:

In late 1940 I was posted as a newly commissioned WAAF officer to Lossiemouth where Sticky was then flying regularly as Station Navigation Officer at the Bomber Command Operational Training Unit of 3 Group.

Almost immediately we fell in love and it was the 'station romance'. We wandered over the nearby golf course during off-duty hours, the peaceful surroundings of sea and Scottish Highlands contrasting with our everyday duties devoted to war training. The 'real' war seemed an age away.

I was rather petite while Sticky was an athletic six-footer.

One senior NCO delighted in travelling between the Navigation Office and mine, delivering notes written in a pseudo-service language arranging rendezvous and other arrangements between Sticky and I. A more incongruous love messenger was difficult to imagine.

I was twenty and Sticky was then twenty-three. The whole station followed and enjoyed our romance with interest and speculation, and soon we became engaged.

Sticky was a professional airman and was bored at the repetitious tasks that he had long mastered. He chafed for the fighting and action, which was the reason for all his training since 1936.

Sticky's philosophy of life was to live it to the fullest, and epitomised the spirit of the day. Life was good for us. Then and much later, when more was involved personally and professionally, I never saw him unhappy.

Two uneventful anti-shipping sorties to the Norwegian coast in Blenheim Mark IV aircraft were flown by Flying Officer Murphy and crews in September 1940.

On 9 November he piloted a Miles Magister with Flying Officer Roach. Sticky recording a forced landing on the Yorkshire moors: 'Trying to get to Yeadon in very bad weather. Got completely lost and had to force land. Put down next to the only visible building I could see, which was a pub. Bang on!'

So well had the art of navigation been absorbed. The advanced courses had not been in vain.

Chapter Five

'The Greatest Fun Ever' – Special Operations on Whitleys and Lysanders

'And now set Europe ablaze!' Such was the order of Prime Minister Winston Churchill when Special Operations Executive (SOE) was formed in August 1940. Clandestine operations were necessary to implement the order. Hitler had conquered France, Belgium and Holland, and planned now to invade Britain. The Battle of, and for, Britain had begun.

Already the Foreign Office operated a system of intelligence gathering by agents who were spies in the traditional sense. Their task was to feed facts to the Government for decisions to be taken. Low profiles in many unexpected roles were essential, and torture and death the likely sole reward.

The task of the SOE was to form and train teams of armed men for sabotage and support of regular troops when the invasion might occur. Captain Buckmaster commanded 'F' (French) Section of the SOE with an outstanding right hand in the person of Section Officer Vera Atkins of the WAAF. The achievements and exploits of this section is well chronicled elsewhere, showing the great contribution to victory not appreciated until war ended.

To produce an effective resistance movement required several years of reinforcement and supply. Trained personnel as instructors and liaison officers had to be dropped or landed from Britain. Control and communication by wireless or despatch presented constant headaches, despite strict selection procedures and training at Beaulieu and other locations.

The few aircraft available meant a struggle to give balanced support in the face of conflicting claims for priority – genuinely impossible to fulfil. To the aircrews engaged, all 'Joes' – as they called their passengers – were equal. Just to be delivered to the target as precisely as was practicable was the aim.

Realising the danger of organised resistance movements, the Germans concentrated on penetration and destruction. Many specialists served in the counter-espionage German Abwehr. Later, the Gestapo – feared and hated because of their vile personnel and methods – reinforced and superseded other branches. The waste of forces in countering national movements became more vital as the Germans were stretched right through Europe.

Further into 1940 and No. 1419 Flight evolved from the embryo No. 419 Special Duty Flight at Stradishall. Their task was support for all clandestine forces within the limits of the small number of hand-picked personnel and the aircraft then available. Armstrong-Whitworth Whitley slab-sided nose-down bombers were used for dropping agents by parachute. The Westland Lysander hopped around with short take-offs and landings, preparing for a routine service of deliveries and pick-ups in Nazi-occupied Europe.

These were early days and Squadron Leader Teddy Knowles commanded No. 1419 Flight at Stradishall when Sticky Murphy arrived in March 1941. Captain Maurice Buckmaster reached the French section of the SOE at about the same time. The main function of the flight was parachuting trained agents – all volunteers – into German-occupied Europe by design and with specific orders. Foreign Office, MI9 and SOE personnel were dropped. Despite reports to the contrary, aircrews often mixed with 'Joes' at Newmarket, Beaulieu and elsewhere. In Sticky's words: 'It was all very cloak and dagger.' Security and secrecy were essential elements.

By the time he was posted to Stradishall, Flight Lieutenant Murphy had flown 857 hours. This included 140 hours of night flying. Sticky had piloted the Anson, Whitley and Blenheim at Lossiemouth and was anxious to test his mettle against the enemy in regular operational sorties. First he flew in a Whitley as second pilot with Squadron Leader Knowles on 12 March 1941. They set out for Prague in Czechoslovakia, but because of delays on take-off had to turn back over Germany after Sticky had navigated them over the centre of Frankfurt. Daylight flying in the slow Whitley over Europe was suicide. Knowles was described as a 'real tough nut'.

It was near Prague that Sticky's great friend of those days – then Flight Lieutenant Ron Hockey – dropped the Czech squad that killed the notorious Heydrich, the 'Butcher of Bohemia'. Dreadful reprisals followed this act, never repeated by the Allies at such a high level of German Command.

Sticky took every opportunity to fly the Westland Lysander, then preparing for the early 'pimpernel' pick-up sorties by Flight Lieutenant John Nesbitt-Dufort. The two became close friends, sharing a light-hearted attitude that masked professional determination. John came to the Special Duty Flight from No. 23 Blenheim Intruder Squadron, where he was briefly acting commanding officer in emergency situations.

No. 1419 Flight moved to Newmarket on 25 May 1941 and agent-dropping sorties continued, with Sticky as second pilot to Squadron Leader Knowles, but after eleven such trips he became captain of his own crew. On the night of 31 August that year, Sticky Murphy commanded the Whitley that dropped 300,000 cigarettes to the Dutch people, to celebrate the birthday of Queen Wilhelmina. In passing he released a stick of bombs on Schiphol (Amsterdam) Aerodrome. On 10 September the King's Flight, commanded by Wing Commander 'Mouse' Fielden, combined with No. 1419 Flight to form No. 138 Squadron. Thus need for greater effort was appreciated, and partly fulfilled, despite setbacks in other theatres of war.

At Newbury, hometown of the bride, on 23 September 1941 at St George's Church, Flight Lieutenant Alan George Michael Murphy and Section Officer Jean Leggat were married. Jean was the daughter of Dr Alexander Gordon Leggat, DSO, a Scottish medical practitioner. The best man, Dennis King, recalled of the occasion:

In 1940 we left the Cottesmore area but kept in touch. The evening of 22 September 1941 was indeed something special as it was Sticky's Bachelor Night party, spent at Hatchetts in Piccadilly – a really good night. It was now that I could see that even with the operational experience he was gaining, it was making no difference to his charm

and friendliness. At St George's Church, Newbury, on the following
day I had the very great privilege of being his best man when he
married Jean Leggat.

There were many other airmen at that wedding, including the
famous 'F for Freddie' Picard. Even though we had had a good stag
night it was possible to enjoy a really wonderful day, which started a
little shakily. While walking my bridegroom across the road to the
church we both stumbled into a ditch, but still managed to get there
without injury and in time. I had cold shivers, thinking I had fluffed
my duty.

We had a good party that night, Sticky, his sister Doreen, and fellow
officers.

This was I think the last time we met, but always his personality,
charm and sincerity will be remembered by all who knew him.

The couple spent a short honeymoon at the Lygon Arms in the beauty
and tranquillity of Broadway, Worcestershire, despite a series of persistent
telephone calls by fellow officers who shared the bridegroom's abundant
sense of humour and joy of boisterous practical jokes. Sticky spent his
twenty-fourth birthday there.

While stationed at Newmarket, the accommodation included various
offices and facilities of the grandstand at Newmarket Racecourse. Flights
were made from these broad, well-kept stretches so ideal for the purpose.
Sticky enjoyed a taste for lobster and any other gourmet food that
appeared in local hotels.

It was a brave man at Newmarket who pulled a toilet chain or got
into his bed without first checking that some explosive device would not
operate when either action took place, courtesy of Messrs Murphy,
Hockey et al. At the same time Sticky was the first to burst into peals of
laughter if the boot was on the other foot. His widow Jean recalled that:

The 'cloak and dagger' period of Sticky's life in its atmosphere of
excitement and dedication, was his great enjoyment to date, particularly
with the Lysander operations that followed. In these latter operations
he was a lone wolf, self-reliant, determined to succeed in the worth-

while aims of landing and collecting brave men and women who penetrated Hitler's Europe, to prepare for the day of liberation. Professionally he was a perfectionist, never content with any second-best performance.

One week after the wedding Sticky flew a night sortie in a Whitley, lasting four hours, and continued other operations during October and November to various parts of France, dropping agents in Toulouse, Tours, Châlons and Limoges as well as other locations in that country.

As John Nesbitt-Dufort made several successful pick-ups and land-ings of agents with his Lysander, with disarming efficiency, those who knew him were impressed. Demands increased for more Lysanders and further collection and delivery. Volunteers included a French pilot in addition to Flight Lieutenant Sticky Murphy and Flying Officer Guy Lockhart from within 'The Firm'. Murphy had proved himself on Whitley sorties and was skilled in night navigation over Europe. Guy Lockhart was a former Spitfire pilot who had been shot down, and while escaping spent a spell in the notorious Miranda internment camp in Spain before returning home via Gibraltar. Squadron Leader Nesbitt-Dufort trained the RAF pilots, as French Flight Lieutenant St Laurent was killed in a new Lysander, together with an expert engine fitter, in a flying accident.

Appendix A gives details of Nesbitt-Dufort's methods and recollections.

Soon the time came for Sticky's first Lysander trip in early December 1941. In separate Lysander aircraft, John and Sticky flew to the advanced operational base at Tangmere, near Chichester on the south coast. John was due for the long slog to Neufchâteau in the Belgian Ardennes, near Luxembourg. His task was to collect Captain Jean Cassart of the Belgian Army – who had been betrayed and was hunted by the Germans as a leader of Belgian Underground efforts. The betrayer had infiltrated his circuit and, as a fellow countryman, was shot by the firing squad after the war for his crime.

John was grounded by the medical officer at Tangmere because of influenza and blocked Eustachian tubes. Sticky volunteered to take his place as his own sortie was cancelled. Thus began the exploit, usually described as the 'Ambush at Neufchâteau' in speculative stories. Not until

1975, when a probing of Belgian historical circles produced the modest Colonel Jean Cassart and a meeting in the Ardennes, could the full tale be told. The discovery of the German report of the event – giving ninety-two soldiers the opportunity to capture or kill Sticky Murphy – filled in some gaps. The meeting with Jean Cassart at Neufchâteau, when his narrative was committed to writing, gave British ears the first version of a remarkable account of heroism to rank with the greatest of the Second World War.

It was then that Colonel (at the time Captain) Cassart heard that John Nesbitt-Dufort was not his fellow participant at Neufchâteau. Now he heard of Squadron Leader Sticky Murphy – whose story he drank in like the wine he shared with the writer and his son Peter in the Ardennes – during the week of John Nesbitt-Dufort's death. John had trained Cassart, code-named 'Captain Metrat', to set out lights in a selected field, and signal identification. The secret code letter 'L' (for Leopold), known only to the two men, was to be flashed from the ground as a security check before landing. Captain Cassart undertook his resistance tasks on instructions from Belgian State Security and SOE. After various security missions he had escaped to England via the Middle East. Following a short training period, Cassart was dropped by parachute into Belgium in August 1941. His remarkable and unique story is recorded in Appendix B. It would be interesting to hear of any other escape from Berlin to London.

Sticky was briefed carefully by Nesbitt-Dufort. Snow was known to blanket his target area, and permission to fly was given only because Cassart was recognised to be in great danger of capture.

He flew off in Lysander T.1508 via Abbeville in northern France and pressed on at 185mph on the two-hour journey to Neufchâteau. The Lysander gave an excellent field of vision to the pilot. An unearthly snow-covered panorama stretched in all directions in the misty moonlight.

Oblivious to the pilot, Jean Cassart waited below for his Stonehenge (see later) and golf-playing friend John Nesbitt-Dufort, and unknown to Cassart, the military police of the German garrisons of Arlon and Namur, mustered to capture the impudent intruder from England and his Belgian comrade. The chosen field had been used by the Luftwaffe in 1940 and was within sight of the town in a dip, with adjoining woods.

A target needing care in daylight it was a formidable exercise to land at
night – much less without the complications of thick snow and mist.
Sticky's laconic note at that time says:

8 December 1941 – Lysander T1508. Five hours and fifteen minutes
night
   flight – TANGMERE–NEUFCHATEAU–TANGMERE.
   Hardly a success. Got there, flew around for an hour, tried to land
on the lights, touched down, saw the flarepath had been laid across a
ditch, opened up again and landed in the middle of the field. There
was bags of moon and snow on the ground. The Huns were, however,
waiting for me and put a number of holes in Languid Lou and one
through my neck. All tanks were hit and got back with 3 gallons. Five
days in hospital and then fourteen days leave. Bang on. Given DFC.

John Nesbitt-Dufort recalled:

I was loath to let Sticky go as I had trained the agent in question.
I gave him the code letter which had to be flashed for recognition
from the ground and was known only to the agent and myself. This
was the letter 'L', which the agent had selected as being the initial of
his king LEOPOLD.
   I could not go to bed despite my condition and went to Control.
As Sticky became due back in the early hours I realised that he was
overdue. Anxiously we awaited some word. The Conducting Officer
of the agent who had come to take him away after landing, was Philip
Rea (Lord Rea, a Liberal peer). We stood by.
   As time passed it was obvious that something serious had happened.
He was long overdue and only one answer seemed possible. Suddenly
a faint call came as I stood beside the Tangmere Controller. The aircraft was plotted with the help of Sticky's broadcast on the VHF radio
telephone. It was clear that his speed was much less than normal
cruising. A weak voice which I could hardly recognise confirmed, by
code, that things had gone wrong. I took the microphone and coaxed
Sticky along, encouraging him to keep going, urging and sustaining
him as he slowly neared home. I realised that he was in dire straits by

the tone of his voice and the surrounding circumstances.

At last Sticky made a perfect landing and without assistance jumped from the aircraft. I could see that he was deathly pale, and on his left shoulder and down his flying suit was a mess, as if someone had poured liquid chocolate over him.

I found that he had been hit on the left side of the neck, tried to stem the bleeding by using my old scarf which he had borrowed, but there was an exit hole as well as an entry in his neck, and he must have been close to unconsciousness for many miles. The aircraft itself was badly shot up, with smoking pieces dropping to the ground after he landed.

Sticky was whisked off to a nearby hospital where I saw him next day, a thorn in the flesh of the administrative and nursing staff, his wife, Jean, having been brought to his side.

As Matron entered his room, Sticky's glass of whisky and bottle disappeared under his bedclothes, but she caught me with a glass in hand, and remonstrated with me, while Sticky had an angelic expression on his face, like a naughty schoolboy. He had complained that the blood transfusion had upset the delicate balance of alcohol in his bloodstream.

Captain Jean Cassart was a graduate of the Belgian Staff College. A man whose panache and personality remained impressive – as did his modesty in 1975 – [he] was in the mould of John and Sticky, from a patriotic point of view. He was organising and training others for military sabotage and resistance in Belgium.

At the meeting in Neufchâteau in September 1975 he demonstrated to the author his clear and vivid recollections of the events in December 1941. How he and two companions made the journey to the pick-up field by car in freezing conditions. His wireless operator and friend, Sergeant Henri Verhagen, was to accompany him to England in the Lysander with a suitcase of documents. A coded BBC message had been received concerning the prehistoric inhabitants of Belgium, and this confirmed the rendezvous.

Suddenly the agents were surrounded by German troops. Shots were fired at Captain Cassart who was wounded in the arm as he escaped, splashing through an icy stream as he climbed a snowy hill before collapsing, exhausted, below the wall of Neufchâteau Cemetery. As the enemy searched for him with powerful torches, the injured Belgian officer heard an aircraft engine overhead. Certain that the pilot would not land without the letter 'L' being signalled, Cassart did not appreciate the sort of man who flew above, orbiting several times and seeking a signal he could read in Morse code.

Sticky Murphy saw many flickering lights and presumed – correctly – that the agent was being chased. Without hesitation he decided that rescue must be tried, regardless of no identifiable signal and possible consequences to himself. He switched on his landing lights as he approached the field, hurdled a ditch that appeared, and landed well down the strip where the enemy had lit the torches to lure him in. The Lysander taxied to a halt in the centre of the field, some distance from the German welcoming party with their machine guns ready.

Only late in 1977 did the German report of their abortive efforts come to light. Appendix C is a detailed translation. In effect, an explanation is given to having lost the intruding aircraft (mis-described), which was riddled with machine-gun fire from thirty metres' range as it took off again. Ninety-two soldiers gathered from the surrounding districts failed to capture or kill Cassart or Murphy.

The chance of seizing these interlopers on German-occupied territory had been lost, and therefore tracing their aerodrome of origin and other information that might be forced from prisoners by well-developed methods – that were later to be tried on Captain Cassart – also eluded them.

Captain Cassart remained undiscovered by the Germans in the thick snow, but awoke to find a Belgian looking down at him from the cemetery wall, saying, 'You must have been cold down there.' Quickly he found that German soldiers filled the town, but were not in the immediate vicinity. The agent made contact with local patriots and returned to Brussels via Liège, only to be betrayed as before.

Cassart spent almost two years in German prisons, with a predictable sequence of starvation and torture, which culminated with companions in a military trial in Berlin. Others who had seen him badly injured in various prisons had slightly exaggerated when they reported that his eyes had been put out and that he was dead. Sentenced to death seven times in one day by the German military court, Jean Cassart stole a cap and spectacles from a workman in the building. He strolled out, saying an enthusiastic 'Heil Hitler' to the challenging guard at the door, and found himself in central Berlin.

After enlisting the aid of French slave labour workers, he walked many miles before finding others, and learned from them that it was possible to travel a limited distance by local trains without confrontation. With the Frenchmen's financial assistance, Jean Cassart reached Brussels with a minimum of delay – a 'stepping-stone' type of journey. There he was whisked away to England once more, stating, 'I have just escaped from Berlin.' Two months of confinement and investigation ensued but, confirmed as a true hero, Cassart pressed to resume the fight, and was promoted, returned to uniform, and again dropped by parachute in the Ardennes, commanding a Belgian unit during the late summer of 1944. His period of German hospitality made him the ideal leader of unorthodox forces freeing his country. His lifestyle was one of modesty and the philosophy to accept life with a smile.

Before being arrested by the Germans in Brussels on 13 December 1941, Captain Cassart and his comrades sent a radio message to London in appreciation of the pilot's brave landing at Neufchâteau, including the words: '… full of admiration for the pilot landing despite the absence of signals. We hope he was not wounded.'

Squadron Leader Sydney Firth, engineering officer, recalled that the Lysander was written off because of the state of airframe and engine.

After suitable consideration by the powers that be, Sticky Murphy was awarded the Distinguished Flying Cross, and on 14 February 1942 No. 161 Squadron was formed, with one flight of Whitleys and one of Lysanders. Now, Sticky still flew the occasional Whitley sortie, but chiefly piloted Lysanders. The squadron was formed from ex-No. 138 Squadron personnel like Squadron Leader Sticky Murphy, with others from the King's Flight. His Majesty's personal pilot, Wing Commander 'Mouse' Fielden, MVO, AFC, commanded No. 138 Squadron.

After his Neufchâteau escapade, it was 27 February 1942 before Sticky, now flying from a base at Graveley, flew another operational trip from Tangmere. On that date he took a woman agent to Saint-Saëns and landed her – expressing his admiration for her courage. 'Must have bags of guts,' he noted. At the same time he collected two 'Joes' and much 'mail'. Operation Baccarat concluded successfully.

[Publisher's note. At this point in the original manuscript a page is missing. The content of the section that we believe is missing will have been within the scope of Appendix D at the end of this book.]

… to their lives, word reached the squadron of his dilemma. Stationmaster Combeau, holder of the Medaille Militaire, the highest French decoration for bravery (won in the First World War), was a courageous and generous host. As his guest waited for weeks, Squadron Leader Nesbitt-Dufort was most conscious of the danger he constituted to the family. Certain death was their reward if discovered by the enemy. After about five weeks 'Brick' and 'St Jacques' returned to Issoudun. The agents announced that a twin-engined aircraft would land soon on a disued airfield nearby. Surprised about a twin being used – hitherto unknown – John realised this was essential because of passengers to be rescued and the distance involved.

General J. Kleeberg, head of the Polish Secret Forces in France from 1940, joined the party of three at the last moment. Almost fifty-three years of age, General Kleeberg was an outstanding Polish soldier and patriot. Five times awarded the Polish Virtuti Militari, he embodied the indomitable Polish spirit and was a leader of his volatile compatriots who respected few persons. He was noted particularly in Polish circles for fighting on in eastern Poland in September 1939 after Warsaw had fallen.

We have the surviving Harry Cossar, DFC – a modest Northumbrian businessman – to thank for his recollection of subsequent events:

I was supposed to be on rest at Newmarket from bomber operations in July 1941 and realised that there were things going on which were highly secret.

Two of my chums in the mess were Johnny Dufort and Sticky Murphy, the latter being a very friendly, pleasant chap who was always laughing and joking.

In early February 1942 I heard that Johnny Dufort had been missing from an operation and Sticky had a quiet word in the mess shortly afterwards and astounded me by saying that he was going to fetch Johnny Dufort by landing in France in an Anson. To cut a long story short, I recovered from my amazement and volunteered to go and we tested an old Anson in which I managed to get wireless and guns fitted and went down to Tangmere in Sussex, from which we flew late on the evening of 1 March 1942 over the snow-covered Continent, having lost our intercommunication in the aircraft because of damage in the turret.

Finally we found the target and Sticky landed the aircraft while I wound down the undercarriage and flaps. Four figures came round the tail as I opened the door, the leading one being Johnny Dufort, who was pointing an automatic pistol straight at my chest. I helped them into the aircraft and after a struggle the old Anson became airborne and eventually we reached Tangmere, all being very thankful to Sticky Murphy for his excellent airmanship. I would have flown to Hell and back with him.

Squadron Leader Murphy's official report of this sortie read:

At 9pm on 1 March 1942 on Operation Beryl II and III, I became air-borne in Anson R.3316 with Pilot Officer Cossar as wireless operator, at Tangmere.

We set course for Cabourg, reached at 22.00 at height of 9,000ft, course then set for Tours. Visibility remained excellent until a point was reached 40 miles north of Tours, when 10/10 cloud encountered with heavy precipitation, visibility in nature of 1,000yd. Some time was spent in pinpointing the Loire and eventually course was set for Châteauroux at 23.15 hours.

Visibility remained poor and I lost myself at 23.30 hours, but eventually reached Châteauroux at 23.55 hours. Course set for Issoudun and light picked up at 00.10 hours.

Landing completed without trouble, and the four passengers embarked very rapidly. We then became airborne again at 00.15 hours and set course for Cabourg. We pinpointed ourselves over the Loire and the Seine and crossed the French coast at Dieppe at 02.00 hours. Course was set for base and we landed at 02.40 hours.

There is an unofficial note in the Operations Record Book of No. 161 Squadron:

The above laconic report marks the completion of a very stout effort both by the pilot and navigator and the Cooks Tourist passenger, but the writer must point out that although the story appears to end at 02.40, at 02.41 hours a party commenced over which a veil has been drawn both by the participants, a select three, and those members of the squadron who were so glad to see our DSO able to use the return half of his ticket.

Squadron Leader Nesbitt-Dufort, accused of smelling like a Paris Metro by Sticky, recorded a note at the time:

We boarded the aircraft without a hitch at high speed. After a hasty conference with the pilot on the advisability of one member of the crew getting out again and pushing to assist the take-off, we decided against this somewhat drastic course, and after eight or nine anxious moments 'Gormless Gertie', the aircraft in question, achieved a speed corresponding to a smart trot, having passed numbers 2 and 3 lights earlier in the evening!

On proceeding at a slightly increased, but rather dangerous speed, we found, to our amazement, that we were airborne. The pilot informed me that if it had not been for the almost previously unheard of, and drastic use of, 'skyhooks', this would undoubtedly not have been accomplished.

The remainder of the trip to base was uneventful, if slow, the skill of the pilot and navigator proved in this case to be exceptional, as we were only lost the majority of the way home, which only goes to show the value of optimism!

Later in March 1942, Nos 138 and 161 Squadrons moved to Tempsford, not far from Bedford, where facilities, aircraft and personnel increased rapidly. The very name became synonymous with the few in the know as a hive of effective clandestine activity.

In October 1974 Colonel Buckmaster wrote:

I would strongly wish to be associated in a tribute to the men of the Royal Air Force who, with tremendous courage and pertinacity, made possible the sending of liaison officers from the United Kingdom to the French Resistance, which, according to the highest authority, had the effect of shortening the war by several months. No praise is too much for their gallantry, devotion and technical skill. All my staff of the French Section of SOE were and are unanimous in their deep appreciation and gratitude to Murphy and his colleagues. The essential need for security in a very perilous game made it impossible to know names but our admiration and respect were unbounded.

At Tempsford Aerodrome was Gibraltar Farm, whose outbuildings helped to camouflage a target that the Germans were anxious to destroy. Tempsford Hall nearby was a large country house where traffic was unobserved.

Squadron Leader Murphy continued to fly further Lysander and Whitley sorties until 29 March 1942 when he received an assessment as a pilot by his commanding officer, Wing Commander 'Mouse' Fielden. It was the rarest compliment – 'Exceptional'. Sticky's own note about the Special Duty operations reads: 'That was the greatest fun ever.'

Only two Lysanders, including John Nesbitt-Dufort's, one pilot and two 'Joes' were lost on missions to France. The Lysander carried two passengers normally, with three at a pinch and four small persons in a desperate emergency, but not on long flights. This aircraft, so much discussed during development for Army cooperation flights, found a historical niche at last. The short take-off and almost helicopter-like landing in skilful and experienced hands proved ideal. Festoons of telephone wire brought back and plenty of foliage from trees often illustrated what close shaves were had in the effort to get off fields of dubious length and terrain.

Murphy and Nesbitt-Dufort were followed by other outstanding pilots of proven courage and ability. These included Wing Commander (later Air Vice Marshal) Sir Alan Boxer, as well as Group Captain 'F for Freddie' Percy Pickard and Group Captain Hugh Verity. Sir Lewis Hodges flew with the greatest distinction behind both the German and Japanese lines on pick-up trips. Wing Commander Wally Farley, who recruited Nesbitt-Dufort, commanded No. 138 Squadron in early days and was lost on operations in 1942. He preceded his old friend John in developing the Lysander techniques. Pickard was lost on the Amiens Prison raid, which released many French Resistance men awaiting execution. Hugh Verity carried out a number of Lysander sorties, sometimes in concert with others in multiple pick-ups. All profited from pioneer tactics and procedures evolved by John and Sticky.

On 19 May 1942, Squadron Leader Murphy, DFC, became a member of the Distinguished Service Order – second only to the Victoria Cross for an officer facing the enemy in wartime. The citation was couched in rather vague terms to conceal his true feats: 'On five recent occasions at night this Officer has carried out operations demanding the highest qualities of skill and organisation. Squadron Leader Murphy has personally organised his Flight and trained his pilots. He has displayed inspiring leadership.'

On 21 April the Free French had previously promulgated the award to Sticky Murphy of the Croix de Guerre with Bronze Palm, by the signature of General Charles de Gaulle, with the citation: 'This very gallant officer has greatly participated in the organisation of operations achieved by Lysander aircraft, for cooperation with the Resistance Movement in France. This officer has accomplished himself, very successfully, [on] a great number of particularly dangerous operations in occupied territory.' This was not such a discreet, but an appreciative, citation.

Sticky Murphy's logbooks show that he had flown a total of 1,350 hours at that time, as he left No. 161 Squadron for a rest from operational flying. He had now carried out thirty-five operational sorties against the 'Blasted Hun'. This was how he described the enemy later, when writing a condolence letter to a widow who had lost her husband in the First World War, and her son under Sticky's command.

Statistics revealed in 1945 that 1,350 parachutists were dropped in France alone from the SOE. Lysanders, Sticky's lone Anson, and later

Dakotas and Hudsons, delivered agents on 250 occasions and brought 450 persons from France clandestinely.

Chapter Six

The Boring Rest at the Air Ministry

With many regrets, late in May 1942 Squadron Leader Murphy left his friends. He was posted as controller to headquarters No. 3 Group, Bomber Command, and then to the Navigation Branch at the Air Ministry. He found that paperwork was still not his forte and to kill time fired missiles at other offices across a main road. 'There I stayed for ten dreary months. I got around quite a bit, however, and flew some new types,' noted Sticky.

New types included a Wicko, Spitfire, Mustang, Puss Moth, Hornet Moth, Stinson and the new and exciting Hawker successor to the Hurricane – namely the Typhoon, destined to be one of the last high-speed propeller-driven single-engined fighters. On 5 March 1943, Sticky flew as second pilot on an anti-submarine patrol in a Sunderland flying boat for more than fourteen hours. He found this rather tedious.

Murphy became so fit and raring to go that he considered non-operational Service extremely boring. He lived in a flat at Notting Hill Gate with Jean and her grand piano, which somehow was lifted to the top floor. This enabled Jean to keep in practice for performances, which pleased so many, as well as accompanied sing-songs that were a feature of many Service parties.

Months passed as Sticky worked hard to obtain a posting of his choice. Wishing to return to operational flying as soon as possible, it was obvious that a squadron command was within his early ambition. His record, and personality, ensured that he could virtually take his pick. Finally he managed to get on the most exciting night-flying operations – Mosquito intruders – preferably in Malta.

Three intruder squadrons existed – Nos 23, 418 and 605. The first was a regular squadron of the Royal Air Force with a long pedigree. In intruder terms, No. 23 was the original RAF squadron, having in 1940 adopted a technique of harassing night flying, which the Germans initially exploited with devastating effect. No. 418 was a Royal Canadian Air Force squadron, and No. 605 an Auxiliary Air Force squadron. Both had successfully emulated No. 23 Squadron's example, operating Boston, Havoc and Mosquito aircraft. There was mutual respect and strong rivalry between the three squadrons.

The command structure was ideal from Squadron Leader Murphy's standpoint. A wing commander as squadron commander was the establishment on a twin-engined fighter-bomber unit, with squadron leaders as flight commanders of each of two flights of nine aircraft, having about twelve crews. Each Mosquito was crewed by a pilot and navigator, the latter also usually a wireless operator.

No. 60 Operational Training Unit (OTU) at High Ercall, near Wellington and Shrewsbury in the county of Shropshire, was the appropriate place for Sticky to train. No. 23 Squadron would need a new flight commander shortly. Paul Rabone, a New Zealander with a long operational record, including as flight commander under John Nesbitt-Dufort on night Beaufighters, was overdue for a rest. He had been involved in suicidal flying of Fairey Battles in France during 1940. It did not escape Squadron Leader Murphy's notice that No. 23 was currently engaged in the most active theatre of war. At Malta in the centre of the Mediterranean the African campaigns were ending, and the invasion of Sicily and Battle of Italy were about to begin.

Group Captain 'Sammy' Hoare, DSO, DFC – 'King of Intruders' – was station commander at the recently formed No. 60 OTU. Formerly a high-scoring pilot and commander of No. 23 Squadron on Blenheims, Havocs, Bostons and Mosquitoes, he was a living legend who continued to fly on operations until the war ended. One eye lost in battle failed to prevent a brilliant career – always flying at night, so that his judgement of distance was remarkable.

A strict commander, this author and his comrades had served under him on Blenheims at No. 51 OTU Twinwood Farm near Bedford, where 'intruding' was formerly taught. At the parent station, Cranfield, night fighters were trained on Blenheims and Beaufighters.

Commanders of training flights at High Ercall were Squadron Leaders Phil Russell, DFC, and Jack Starr, DFC. These pilots served on No. 23 Squadron at Ford in late 1942, and flew with the squadron to Malta at the end of December that year, operating with distinction from that island. They were flight commanders under Wing Commander Peter Wykeham-Barnes, DSO, DFC.

Pleased to be flying again, Sticky's first task, apart from mastering the de Havilland Mosquito, was to find a navigator. He 'crewed up' (often a procedure more important than getting married) with Flying Officer Jock Reid, who remembered:

It was about the second week of June 1943 that I met Squadron Leader Murphy in the mess at High Ercall. We had moved there from Twinwood Farm in Bedfordshire where I had been a navigation instructor. I was looking for a pilot and he was looking for a navigator. We teamed up and I flew with him throughout his conversion to the Mosquito, and then on the course. I was most impressed by his ability as a pilot, and soon had the utmost confidence in him. He was an excellent pilot, and as I thought my ability as a navigator was not bad, I felt very confident. Right from the beginning of our partnership Sticky never questioned that ability. He did what I requested pertaining to navigation, and although we had some disagreement about what, how and when to attack, we usually arrived at a fair compromise. OTU training was a period of adjustment. I weighed him up, and I suppose he did the same.

The history of intruding, with various ploys, was taught by instructors on rest from operational squadrons – Nos 23, 418 and 605. At High Ercall 'orbiting the firkin Wrekin' (as the local RAF song went) referred to the humpbacked hill resembling a whale, called 'The Wrekin', which overlooked the airfield and commanded a panoramic view, but was a hazard on dark nights as it was on the approach leg when certain winds blew.

Phil Russell quickly showed Sticky Murphy the form on the Mosquito, which produced a solo flight on 24 June 1943 after an hour's instruction. After carrying out the prolonged series of navigation, bombing and gunnery exercises, with attacks at low level on ground targets and air-to-air firing, Sticky received an assessment in his logbook of 'Exceptional on course'. Jack Starr was his assessor.

Squadron Leader Murphy had the support and cooperation, not to mention the capable navigation, of the rather dour Jock Reid, a flying officer and a Scot, who hid his sense of humour for appropriate moments. They were felt to be a good team. Jock's caution and common sense balanced Sticky's exuberant, aggressive attitude towards the enemy.

After embarkation leave they met at RAF Lyneham near Swindon – the transit aerodrome from which a new Mosquito Mk VI was to be collected at nearby Kemble. Petrol consumption tests had to be carried out on a long nationwide patrol. Nothing would be more futile than to drop an expensive aircraft, and even more expensive crew, into the Bay of Biscay on the way to Gibraltar because of an unknown fault. While there, Jock had a personal emergency, and obtained compassionate leave. Sticky flew him to High Ercall for onward transfer to Scotland.

Jock recalled a conversation with Sticky when they were going to sleep in their billet at Lyneham. Sticky described his dream of war in the days of chivalry, when only personal fitness, nerve, endurance and skill counted for survival. Man-to-man combat with a sword, with no machines or guns; a knight in shining armour was the aspect that captured Sticky's imagination. The caparisoned horses, rules, ritual and chivalrous qualities appealed to him. This was another side of his personality – confident and aggressive, eager to test his mettle, again and again, against the elements and the enemy.

Sticky found a temporary navigator – Flight Lieutenant Bilbe-Robinson – to join him in his flight to No. 23 Squadron in Malta. They shared the flight on 23 September 1943 from Portreath in Cornwall via the Bay of Biscay to Gibraltar. En route Sticky noted: 'An hour after take-off we were jumped by eight Me 110s. By crafty use of much boost and many revs, we managed to hit some cloud before they got within range. Flew over some of Spain and Portugal.'

His orders were to fly to Gibraltar without loitering on the way. This flight took five hours and twenty minutes, and the check on the port wing side for land was the instinctive navigation ploy – with all the water of the Atlantic Ocean off the starboard wing!

Then followed a flight for about an hour to Oujda in Algeria, followed next day to Luqa on Malta GC for over four hours to the reception described in the opening of this book. It was 24 September 1943. Sticky and 'Bilbe' were conveyed in an old American car to the Meadowbank Hotel, which was the officers' mess at Sliema on the seafront, just west of Grand Harbour and Valletta.

Chapter Seven

No. 23 Squadron's History – 1915–September 1943

No. 23 Squadron of the Royal Flying Corps was formed at Gosport near Portsmouth on 1 September 1915. The first duties of the new squadron were night patrols to combat Zeppelin bombing raids on London – so damaging to civilian and Service morale. Night flying was in a state of infancy.

Second Lieutenant John Slessor – very much a fledgling, but destined, despite polio damage at an earlier age, to become Marshal of the Royal Air Force as Sir John Slessor, GCB, DSO, MC – was at that time one of the pioneer pilots in this field. In his classic autobiographical book *The Central Blue*, he tells of his early efforts on No. 23 Squadron when he hunted an elusive Zeppelin L.15 over London on 13 October 1915. This first night interception was watched by many thousands, when the climbing power of the aircraft was less than the escaping power of the airship, whose commander cut his engines and listened for his pursuer before departing without ceremony. Many years later Slessor and the Zeppelin commander discussed their recollections and tactics.

The first battle honour of the squadron was 'Home Defence 1916', and the eagle (signifying the most powerful of air fighters) is shown on the squadron crest, together with the motto 'Semper Aggressus', usually translated as 'Always on the attack'.

A long line of distinguished airmen as commanding officers was led by Captain Louis Strange, a man of outstanding personality and character from Dorset, recalled with affection and admiration in later years by Sir John Slessor as 'A delightfully irrepressible and fearless officer.'

Another comrade, Lieutenant Harry Kelly, was remembered as 'A brilliant and fearless pilot, wild as a hawk, with a very irreverent sense of humour.'

Both descriptions also aptly described a later commanding officer of No. 23 Squadron – Wing Commander Alan 'Sticky' Murphy.

On 16 March 1916, No. 23 Squadron landed in France as part of the expanding air arm, and the commanding officer of their wing was Lieutenant Colonel C.F Murphy (no relation). Now fighting and bombing by day was the squadron's role, despite night interception and intruding being the main function throughout the two world wars.

Captain Strange became lieutenant colonel (equivalent to the Royal Air Force rank of wing commander) and was decorated with the Distinguished Service Order, Military Cross and the Distinguished Flying Cross as he waged what seemed to be almost a one-man war against the Germans in various ways. Certainly there are few records of a man so devoted to ending hostilities as soon as possible. For example, on 22 April 1915 he spotted the first sign of the green cloud of gas that drifted on a beautiful evening from the German lines towards the French positions and overwhelmed the Allies, leaving the way open to Ypres.

When a captain on No. 6 Squadron on 10 May 1915, Strange fought a German aircraft using a Lewis machine gun fitted to the front cockpit of his Martinsyde Scout. They both withdrew to change ammunition drums before resuming the contest. During this task Strange's aircraft became inverted and spun for 3,000 feet. The dangling pilot hung on to the gun and rear centre strut and somehow managed to right his plane and fly it home.

On another occasion he successfully killed many German reinforcements at Courtrai railway station as he attacked with bombs from point-blank range at low level. In the course of this assault he silenced a German soldier who was shooting at him by throwing a hand grenade. 'Semper Aggressus' indeed!

His technical bent and determination involved Captain Strange in the earliest bombsight construction and tests, apart from experiments that led to machine guns replacing rifles and revolvers. The 'modern' methods of warfare then continued for at least a further sixty years.

In October 1916, Second Lieutenant G.J. Ogg of No. 23 Squadron made his mark on the history books by landing his aircraft after a fight with five of the enemy. He was an observer whose pilot had been mortally wounded in combat, and Ogg was awarded the Victoria Cross.

During the Second World War Louis Strange was in France as a pilot officer and was given a Bar to his Distinguished Flying Cross for bringing home a Hawker Hurricane fighter that he had repaired and flown. It was his first flight in a modern aircraft. Later, as a wing commander he became commanding officer of the Central Landing School, where glider pilots and paratroops went for training, and the airborne forces received the benefit of his experience, personality and panache.

The battle honour 'Ypres 1917' was awarded to No. 23 Squadron in recognition of the offensive spirit against enemy aircraft and ground installations during that dreadful epic. The final battle honour, 'Somme 1918', was granted in the closing stages of the First World War.

Disbanded soon after, but re-formed in 1925 under the command of Squadron Leader Collishaw, DSO, OBE, DSC, DFC – the 'Canadian Ace' of the First World War, who had the third highest total of British kills – No. 23 Squadron carried on with the élan of earlier days. Collishaw, too, continued to fight the enemy into the 1940s as an air chief marshal, and was renowned for courage, drive and formidable leadership.

Flying competitions were lively events with other squadrons for trophies during the 1930s, maintaining the high standard of airmanship. The close aerobatic display by Flight Lieutenant Day and Pilot Officer Douglas Bader at Hendon in 1931, brought warm appreciation of their skills and further recognition of the squadron's quality. It was on No. 23 Squadron that the later Group Captain Sir Douglas Bader, CBE, DSO, DFC, had his serious accident that preceded his exploits so well chronicled in his biography and film *Reach for the Sky*.

Wing Commander 'Wings' Day was one of the earliest casualties in a hopeless daytime Blenheim sortie during 1940, and proved an inspiration in prisoner-of-war camps to escapers. He made numerous attempts and actual escapes before surviving unspeakable conditions in concentration camps with a broken body but indomitable spirit. His biography, *Wings*, by Sydney Smith, stirs the emotions of the hardest cynic by the depths plumbed without surrender to the hate tyranny he experienced more than most. He epitomised the Royal Air Force spirit.

In September 1935 the squadron flew Demons to Malta in connection with the Italian invasion of Ethiopia, but no action followed. The British Government and League of Nations again waffled and surrendered to aggression, bringing closer and more certain the Second World War.

During the early days of conflict, No. 23 Squadron was used in night defence, earning the battle honour 'Channel and North Sea 1939–40'. Late in 1940 the secret black boxes known as AI (Aircraft Identification) Mk I were fitted to the Blenheim aircraft. This was the earliest airborne radar detection equipment to fight enemy raiders.

'Intruding' – the technique of harassing enemy aircraft by patrolling in the vicinity of base aerodromes – was a German idea. It was an eerie feeling to know that enemy planes were lurking in darkness waiting to pounce with guns and bombs. In returning bombers, wounded men, aircraft damage or shortage of fuel, made a quick landing imperative.

In terms of aircraft destroyed, aerodromes bombed and impairment to crew morale, incalculable harm was done. The Germans made effective intruder sorties over England during 1940 and 1941, where frantic efforts were made to train aircrews to maintain defence over the country and offence over occupied Europe.

In mid-October 1941, Hitler arbitrarily withdrew permission for intruder operations – despite their success. 'The German people must see the proof of victories over the Fatherland', was his order. This was another grave error. Targets for intruders over England were increasingly juicy and tempting. Training elements, as well as aircraft on missions, abounded by now in the day and night skies. Apart from the obvious vulnerability in trainers, operational aircraft were also at risk when heavily laden with bombs and fuel. Taking off in this state, or staggering home with little fuel, was a twitchy business.

No. 23 Squadron became the first intruder squadron of Fighter Command, attacking airfields in north-west France, Holland and Belgium where enemy bombers then proliferated. Bristol Blenheim fighter-bombers, both Mks I and IV, were not ideal for this role, for which the Junkers Ju 88s were used by the Luftwaffe. With experience, improved techniques evolved. Later, Douglas Boston and Havoc fighter-bombers came to No. 23 Squadron, and it was over this switchover that the acting squadron commander, Flight Lieutenant John Nesbitt-Dufort, departed from the scene. The senior officer who insisted that Bostons should be launched that night against German airfields, refused to listen to John's explanation that conversion of fuel tanks must be completed first. The aircraft were still sent off, with resultant waste of crews and aircraft.

The Bostons, like the Blenheims, were painted black and operated with increased range and versatility during 1941 and 1942, attacking airfields, marshalling yards and similar targets.

A new era dawned on 2 July 1942 when the first Mosquito reached No. 23 Squadron, and intruding became increasingly the 'offence' part of the motto of Fighter Command ('Offence Defence'). Many tactics continued to be evolved to fox the enemy and attack his aircraft, or cause them to crash out of fuel. It was a long way from the 'gallantry' of the histories of air war in earlier days. Ambush, hunting and psychological pressure were involved. The tide had turned in air warfare – despite set-backs and disasters on land and at sea.

Bomb-carrying capacity, and the use of four 20mm cannon with increased-range capability, strengthened the squadron's efforts. The Mk II Mosquito was the first fighter-bomber of the type, evolved from the Mk IV light bomber that had made history with the swoop in daylight on Oslo.

Later, the more powerful Mk VI with advanced technology, carrying the same Hispano cannon and four .303-inch machine guns, managed to convey two 500lb bombs in the rear belly and one of the same under each wing. No. 23 Squadron, and now also No. 605 Auxiliary and No. 418 Royal Canadian Air Force Squadrons, ranged the German night skies with increasing success. German scientists responded to the multiple ploys by lighting false, heavily defended, decoy airfields, with other countermeasures that demonstrated the effectiveness of the RAF effort. Mine layers and bombers were attacked, with the low-level flying at night essential for intruding. No radio altimeters to register height above passing ground, and no airborne radar for interception or direction-finding, made it something of a pencil and paper 'instinctive' navigation exercise on dark nights. Sir Isaac Newton's 'gravity' was ever present to entrap strafing or overenthusiastic crews.

At Ford, near Chichester on the Sussex coast, Wing Commander 'Sammy' O'Bryen Hoare, DSO, DFC – the 'King of Intruders' who had flown Blenheims, Bostons, Havocs and the first Mosquito Mk II on No. 23 Squadron – was replaced in September 1942. Wing Commander Peter Wykeham-Barnes, DFC, a veteran of many theatres of war including the Desert, Greece and Norway, became squadron commander. A Halton 'brat' by Service origin, who gained special entry to Cranwell as a flight cadet, he finally retired in 1976 as Air Chief Marshal Sir Peter Wykeham, KCB, DSO, OBE, DFC, AFC. Rapidly taking to intruder sorties, he was carrying out operational flying as late as the Korean War. A daring and resourceful leader in the tradition of No. 23, he assumed command at a vital time in the squadron's history.

As day bombing was reduced substantially by the Spitfire and other reinforcements on the island of Malta during 1942, night bombing continued in abundance. The need for an intruder force to harass the enemy night bombers from Sicilian and Italian bases, resulted in No. 23 Squadron suddenly flying to Luqa, Malta GC, at the end of 1942 – first operating before that fateful year ended. The attachment from Fighter Command was to be for three months, but old sweats had heard that story before.

Apart from intruding on enemy bomber bases, support was given to the Desert Air Force by strafing and bombing attacks on the crowded roads of North Africa. Victory at El Alamein had been achieved at last. As Rommel's Afrika Corps reached Libya and Tunisia in retreat, No. 23 Squadron was at hand. Twice nightly sorties helped to speed the Axis forces on their way. The exploits of Wing Commander Wykeham-Barnes and his aggressive crews were well remembered in Malta more than thirty years later. Nightly they threatened, checked and destroyed the night bombers that had been so persistent. Luftwaffe sorties reduced in number as intruders made bases too dangerous for nightly forays.

Malta had survived the plans of the German High Command for invasion in Operation Hercules. Despite orders to invade by sea and air, Field Marshal Kesselring gradually dropped the idea. Goering was not in favour. He remembered too well the fierce resistance of British and New Zealand troops defending Crete in a similar invasion. Crippling losses to the airborne troops of General Student now produced a dividend. As Malta's garrison of all three Services switched gradually to the offensive and were spared invasion, it was clear that Crete's defenders had played their part well in Malta's defence too.

Regarded as 'indefensible' by British 'experts' before the Second World War, the island remained the lynchpin of the Mediterranean theatre. Command of the sea of that name, or 'Our Sea' as the Italians preferred, would have been lost with disastrous consequences, and history would have recorded a different and difficult time for the Allies.

Blenheim bombers of No. 107 Squadron, as well as Wellingtons and others, with sacrifice worthy of highest praise, earlier attacked supply ships and tankers for the Afrika Corps. They made Malta a repeatedly stinging hornet, and ensured that Rommel and his forces never received the fuel and supplies needed for operational efficiency. 'A dagger at Hitler's throat' was another description of Malta's role. Air Vice Marshal Sir Hugh Pughe Lloyd had commanded RAF Malta in 1941 and was succeeded by the operational commander of the vital No. 11 Group during the Battle of Britain, the charming and most able Air Vice Marshal Sir Keith Park. The concern for his crews of this New Zealander, a veteran soldier of Gallipoli and airman of the First World War, and his experienced command, ensured that no effort was wasted. Best use of precious petrol delivered by submarine and heavily attacked tanker, was assured.

A plateau rose gently from the centre of Malta, breaking the panorama of ancient buildings and villages. Phoenicians and other travellers founded the community on the island and suffered repeated conquest by varying invaders over a period of 2,000 years. Already in ancient times the group of Maltese islands stood strategically in the centre of the 'Sea of the Middle of the Known World'. Later they were caught between the armed might of Rome and Carthage. Saint Paul was shipwrecked at St Paul's Bay on his journey to captivity in Rome. Many valiant deeds were recorded throughout Maltese history, including the epic siege of the Turkish armies and resistance by the Knights of Malta during the seventeenth century.

Here on the main island, aircrews had a few hours' rest during 1943, where, on this plateau Luqa Aerodrome was the home of swarms of Allied aircraft that rose to attack the Axis forces. Fore and aft, the plateau was bounded by a ravine (usually called 'the wadi') and a quarry where the subterranean administrators of the Royal Air Force carried out their tasks. The aerodrome was ideal for both day and night operations, now that the Luftwaffe and Regia Aeronautica had lost their erstwhile command of the skies. The heroic defence of Malta during 1940–42 has been well reported elsewhere, not least by Captain Ron Gillman, DFC, DFM, in *The Shiphunters*. Sinking Rommel's supply ships in 1941, the Blenheims and their crews were as expendable as the Mosquitoes and their aircrews a year and more later.

In early July 1943, the war zone moved from Africa to the island of Sicily. No. 23 Squadron intruded on German bases as well as bombing and strafing searchlight and flak positions likely to interfere with the airborne landings by parachute and glider. Many of the pilots towing from North Africa were inexperienced and unused to searchlights and flak. They cast off their charges way off the coast of Augusta and Syracuse to perish in the sea, and therefore destroyed highly trained troops and the opportunity to end the German resistance on the Plain of Catania – the road to Messina and metropolitan Italy. The excellent start to the Sicilian campaign with General George Patton driving his troops forward in competition with the victorious General Montgomery, promised much, and after two months succeeded.

No. 23 Squadron then moved forward to bases on the Plain of Catania at Sigonella and Gerbini Main – mud strips, but flat. Now they saw the reality of sabre-toothed mountains and the savage terrain that moonlight had bathed with a benevolent glow on night sorties. Also they saw the aftermath of ground war in the cairns of stones as temporary graves in the vicinity of Parachute Bridge where next day the boots had been stolen from the hastily covered casualties of both sides.

Instead of the 2s 6d per egg they had to pay on the Maltese black market, Sicily was the source of ample eggs, lemons, oranges and other food. Morale improved with better diet, although the old tins of Eighth Army stews continued for some time, with occasional bully beef as a treat.

By this time Wing Commander John Selby, DSO, DFC, had taken over from Wykeham-Barnes, who had had a shaky flight home to England with Squadron Leader Phil Russell, DFC, also tour-expired after outstanding operational exploits. Selby was a Desert Air Force veteran, who on one occasion took General 'Boy' Browning, commander of British airborne forces, on an early reconnaissance of Sicilian landing and dropping zones in the moonlight. In the same way, he flew Air Vice Marshal Sir Keith Park

on night reconnaissance. Squadron records show that he told the
general (the husband of novelist Daphne du Maurier): 'Never mind the
view. Keep your eyes out the back for bloody fighters.' A veteran of Sir
Keith Park's Service would have needed no such injunction.

In September 1943, Wing Commander Selby was succeeded by Wing
Commander Peter Burton-Gyles, DSO, DFC, a dark-haired youthful, shy
but experienced pilot from Britain. Word came back to the squadron
that Selby had volunteered for hazardous tasks, trained as a parachutist
in Palestine, and then joined the Yugoslavs of Tito's partisans with
Winston Churchill's son Randolph and others as a liaison officer. His
arrival was effected by submarine! 'Semper Aggressus' indeed.

Within less than one year, No. 23 Squadron was 'controlled' by Fighter,
Coastal and Bomber Commands, but remained a very independent air
force with Australian, Belgian, Canadian, New Zealand and Polish airmen
blending harmoniously, with a predominance of United Kingdom
personnel. They carried on the traditions in the knowledge that it was
a privilege to serve on such a squadron, whose élan and determination
to work and play hard are still remembered in areas where they served
– not the least on Malta.

The 'Whispering Death' Bristol Beaufighter and a few Mosquitoes of
No. 256 Squadron from England attacked, with AI now advanced in
design, the few night raiders now assaulting Malta. These attacks were
pinpricks compared with earlier nights, but the over-tried civilian population's morale was seriously impaired – starved as they were – with
signs of malnutrition everywhere.

No. 23's intruder role had earlier expanded to train busting, by strafing
trains in motion and at rest, as well as targeting railway stations and
individual engines in Sicily and Italy. The offensive patrols satisfied
that aggressive spirit frustrated by the reduction of German Air Force
activities. The battle honour 'North Africa 1943' was awarded for the
efforts from Malta.

High-flying reconnaissance aircraft ventured overhead occasionally
by day. Night bombing was being reduced by the war of attrition waged
by night fighter, bomber and intruder crews. Malta hit back with a
vengeance. The battered huts of galvanised iron and wood patchwork –
more suitable for public lavatories in a banana republic – bore eloquent

witness to past battles. They served the squadrons who revenged their outnumbered predecessors.

Operational flying was a hard school. There was no room for sentiment. All crews were volunteers – probably anyone could opt out. Possibly there was a procedure for this, but it was not known, and this was just as well. No person in his right mind would continue to throw himself into the nightly elements of danger, apparently unending until death or disappearance supervened. 'Tours of operation' were occasionally completed. The number of set sorties varied. Thirty to fifty trips was the span of a tour.

The isolation of two men in such close proximity, with radio speech seldom interrupting, was a privileged moment in timeless space. Until some hundreds of miles had been travelled at more than four miles a minute, only the automatic searching of instruments, checking of fuel consumption etc., interrupted the mood. Suddenly, however, a patch of turbulent air would put both men on the 'qui vive' (lookout), with a rapid manoeuvre and search for the reason – often the slipstream of a friendly aircraft – that swiftly brought them back to reality. If the aircraft was found, as sometimes happened, a close inspection was made (clear of known gun positions), to confirm identification, before slipping away and leaving a possible target unsuspecting. They appeared so vulnerable from the traditional night attack position, looking up into the belly.

The Maltese islands of Malta, Gozo and Comino are situated at the closest point 58 miles from Sicily and 180 miles from North Africa, with Gibraltar 1,141 miles to the west and Alexandria 944 miles to the east. The island of Malta is about 17 miles in its longest straight distance and 9 miles wide, with Gozo about half of these dimensions.

The native population of approximately 300,000 was swollen by the British Services, without whom the island would have been conquered long ago. The capital of Valletta and its Grand Harbour proved to be an ideal port for the warships of the Royal and Merchant Navies for many years. A relationship had been established in peacetime between the British Services and the Maltese people, a number of whom served in the Royal Navy. Many daughters had become brides of Britons.

The Maltese people were bilingual, English being their second language, and the ancient Maltese tongue – a distinct language with a Semitic structure – was enhanced by foreign additions and assimilations. In appearance they had much in common with the southern Italian and Sicilian peoples. Italian was understood by most Maltese, with the use of Latin in religious observances. The Roman Catholic Church ruled the civilian administration and population with an inexorable grip. The sea surrounding Malta was perfect for fishing and swimming, and the volatile Maltese led a vigorous social life. Sliema, where No. 23 Squadron aircrews were billeted, was the largest and most modern town in Malta with a fashionable residential area. It was a noted resort with a two-mile-long seafront promenade. This was crowded in the evenings, even at the height of the 'bombing season', unless bombs were actually falling. Britons who had suffered the German blitz campaign in England were somewhat surprised to see the rather excited and noisy scampering of the Maltese people when sirens sounded on the much-battered island. Later they considered this stolid compared with the crowds who ran hysterically in all directions when the German Air Force attacked the Port of Naples.

During early days in Malta, when they had the energy, a number of pilots and observers played water polo. On one occasion, off the rocks of Sliema a few yards from the billet 'Casa Leone', a pilot had been taught to swim by the others. He was improving his 'dog paddle' breast stroke by the edge in four or five feet of water. Others were enjoying the chase and tackles of water polo. His observer looked for his pilot and saw the sea calm and empty, and the rocks were bare. He presumed he had gone to the billet. An impulse made him swim towards the rocks. He noticed something like a piece of seaweed or an octopus below the surface. Octopuses were plentiful in that area, but he grasped the object in his right hand in a moment of inspiration. Up came the red-faced head of the pilot whose hair it had been.

Quickly telling the pilot to relax, he took the drowning man by the cupped ears in the approved method of the Royal Life Saving Society. The pilot did as he was told – and sank like a stone in a vertical position. The observer held on grimly as the descent (which he was unable to prevent) continued … and continued … until finally he reached the seabed at about fifteen feet, sprang off the bottom, and made the return journey upwards to eventually break the surface. The observer dared not let go of the pilot, despite bursting lungs, as he was clearly full of water already. A shout to a nearby comrade helped to pull the pilot on to the rocks and pump the water from him. More than thirty years later, the three men discussed this episode and had similar vivid recollections of the incident.

Soon after the Sicilian campaign ended the Italians surrendered, quickly followed by Operation Avalanche – the Allied invasion of metropolitan Italy at the Bay of Salerno. This place is best described as being on the shin of the Italian 'foot', just south of the Bay of Naples and the Sorrento Peninsula. No. 23 Squadron was busily engaged that night until first light, intruding on the aerodromes north of Rome called Grosseto and Viterbo. It was known that these were the bases of bomber and torpedo-bomber aircraft. The German crews had the opportunity of their lives to attack the huge invasion fleet. For twenty-four hours before the actual landing, ships were spread across the Mediterranean as far as the eye could see towards the western edge of Sicily.

Luqa at this time held a multiplicity of aircraft. Wellingtons for bombing, torpedoing, submarine search and destroy missions, dwarfed the Martin Baltimores and Douglas Boston light bombers of the Desert Air Force. From neighbouring Ta' Qali and Safi rose the day fighter-bomber squadrons of Spitfires, Kittyhawks and similar. Many of the ground crews of No. 23 had served in the Western Desert campaigns and coped in a superb manner in enervating scorching heat, with the maintenance of aircraft in primitive and unexpected circumstances. They were veterans in the best sense of the word. Many others had come from England, following the aircrews who had flown the Mosquitoes from the United Kingdom. Steve Ruffle was one – who served at Ford, Luqa, Alghero and later again in England, as did Douglas Higgins, the squadron artist under five COs.

One of the outstanding aircrews by contrast, both physical and psychological, were Shorty Dawson and Fergie Murray – pilot and navigator of a Mosquito for months past, who had knitted into an exceptional operational unit.

Sergeant Shorty Dawson, Australian to the core, was five feet two inches tall, with a fine physique and the coolest temperament. By this time he had ceased to consider his mates as 'Pommies', but strangers from Britain were still 'Poms'. To be a pal of Shorty's was to find a generous friend, constantly puzzled by English customs, but with the warmest of personalities. His passion was an iniquitous game with two coins tossed in the air. 'Two up' he called it, and gambled from Australia to the United Kingdom on the ship that brought hundreds of trained airmen in support of the Mother country. Shorty proudly showed photographs of the 'two up schools' on board, with himself holding a fistful of bank-notes. This was sufficient warning to those tempted to tangle with him in his national game. He had a dry and penetrating wit.

Fergie Murray was ten years older than the others, and a man of passionate beliefs, emotional temperament and iron determination. A devoted married man, the squarely built Londoner was of medium height, with greying hair, and a corpulence that quickly disappeared in Malta. An ebullient character, he was the 'old man' in training. Only the younger airmen who had seen him, teeth out and fists flying, quelling bullies on the rugby field, fully appreciated his qualities.

During August 1943 there had been an epidemic of engine failures and single-engined performances that had ended in fatalities – among those whose fate was known. Jack Farrelly – an ex-Sheffield City police-man – with his temporary navigator Louis 'Squeege' Sabine – a former bank clerk from Reigate and a Territorial soldier who had served with the Queen's Regiment in France – had been killed. Jack had been trained at Twinwood Farm OTU with Sticky's reception committee. 'Squeege' had been trained with the navigators since 1941 and was keen to combat the enemy on more even terms than a rifle and bayonet against tanks.

In the higher echelons something shifted – Geoffrey de Havilland, chief test pilot of the Mosquito throughout its development, came to Malta. Feathering one engine after take-off from Luqa, he performed a roll while climbing off the deck, then threw the aircraft around the sky and landed – indicating that all it required was more efficient piloting. Shorty Dawson, later to be a test pilot for many months, was most unimpressed.

Jeez,' said Shorty, never a respecter of persons, 'now put 600 gallons of juice on board, fill up with cannon and machine-gun ammunition and do all that again!'

'Not likely,' replied the famous man.

'What about the overheating on the engine when one has gone,' remarked Shorty.

'Dive – that will cool it', was the answer.

'What, from flaming 200 feet on the other side?' retorted Shorty.

There was no audible response. The problem of losing power or performance on engines on fire remained. The expert returned to the United Kingdom where air temperatures were more suitable.

Losing an engine was discussed among the crews. When 600 miles from base or friendly territory it was rather difficult. The offending engine usually failed immediately after a low ground strafing attack on a train or aerodrome. Little sympathy was likely if a crash-landing had to be made nearby. Theories abounded on such misfortune – one being that the plastic caps on machine-gun muzzles pierced the glycol tank. Shorty's 200-foot trouble at Foggia and miracle landing at Palermo in Sicily involved three hours' flying on one engine through 4,000-foot valleys of 8,000-foot-high mountains in the moonlight. The lights of two Jeeps showed the pocket-handkerchief-sized aerodrome for touchdown, as balloons in the harbour and mountains on the fourth side were somehow evaded.

Squadron Leader Paul Rabone borrowed a Spitfire in Malta and flew to Palermo, being forced to overshoot due to the size of the field. On his return journey he shot down a Junkers Ju 88!

Shorty and Fergie found that a bolt under the carburettor had shaken loose during vibration caused by the cannonade. Fuel drained off and the engine failed. At least the reason was established. By unloading guns and using their 'aerobatic take-off technique' the crew got airborne in a minimum distance – to the surprise of the United States Spitfire pilots who had been excellent hosts. The crew had numerous arguments, and told how Fergie was praying and Shorty swearing through the moonlit valleys.

In discussion afterwards about this remarkable journey, Fergie said: 'I did not know half the words he was using when he was swearing!'

Shorty replied: 'Well I did not know what you were talking about when you were praying, but I didn't care.'

They revelled in this sort of acrimonious discussion and raked up old scores and differences, which only showed how closely bound they were by shared experience.

Urged on by comrades at Cranwell's School of Signals and No. 6 Air Observers' Navigation School, Fergie Murray continued to pass severe tests – made more problematic by his age. A Roman Catholic – subject to the archaic shout on Sundays in the Service – 'Fall out Jews, Roman Catholics and others' – Fergie was a constantly cheerful friend, counsellor and wit. Because of a minor disability he was to be parted from men who had been with him since 1941, but fought Medical Boards to accompany them, and won. The medical pundits were surprised to find a man of his age so determined to go into the thick of the war, when they presumed he was anxious to go in the other direction.

Fergie had lost 28lb in weight on Malta rations, but was still a Churchillian-type bulldog of a man, with a background as a commercial traveller. He could not drink and must have been the original 'sniff of a barmaid's apron' fellow.

The more he and Shorty fought and argued, the closer they became. 'Jeez, Ferg,' said Shorty, 'what are you whingeing on about now? I've never met such a whinger. Go and get in your pit, an old bastard like you needs plenty of sleep.'

'Who was it went to sleep over the Bay of Biscay, you saucy sod?' replied Fergie. 'Spent half the night God knows where, lost your posh watch, we had to take off at dawn, and you just got back in time! Why didn't I get a proper pilot instead of an Aboriginal short-arse?'

Shorty always brought this sort of friendly chat to a rapid end by saying: 'What about a game of "two up" Ferg?'

On which cue Fergie fled, remarking to the others: 'He's such a good pilot really, but won't stop arguing.'

Shorty was invisible to passers-by when taxiing a Blenheim or Mosquito. It became a standing joke that when a shout arose, then an aircraft was running away with no pilot. 'It's OK, Shorty is the invisible man again', was the cry. With Fergie he evolved an aerobatic take-off from short runways in a Mosquito. This required absolute mutual confidence. They counted to four after eighty-five knots appeared on the airspeed indicator, and at Shorty's signal Fergie put down the flap lever. The Mosquito then made an elevated early take-off – unorthodox and dangerous, but most effective, and, on at least one special occasion, essential.

Two instances of the type of leadership before Squadron Leader Murphy's arrival on 24 September 1943 are recalled. One crew had a tyre burst on take-off, giving an easy alternative to a fiery death by hitting a pillbox dead ahead if the 'book' was followed, or landing in the quarry to the starboard with a loud bang, and disturbing the wing commander (administration) and other 'denizens'. A third option was chosen – flying speed being miraculously achieved by using emergency boost on both engines. The lurch to starboard when that side's tyre burst was arrested. Shakily the Mosquito staggered into the air, where it found that the oleo leg on that side had been damaged, the jack bent so no retraction possible. A crash was inevitable. In the midday heat, with 600 gallons of juice aboard, this was not an encouraging prospect, but after reducing weight by strafing the islet of Filfla to expend cannon and machine-gun ammunition, the attempt was made.

With great skill, the sergeant pilot cut the switches and pulled up the undercarriage as the starboard bent leg collapsed soon after touching down. The stricken kite, HJ 739, slewed to a halt, but was undamaged enough to be repaired and flown again. It was a stout effort, and rations for ground and aircrews in Sicily were salvaged. No fire ensued, except from the crew, when a clown of a senior officer – not from the squadron – appeared and berated the pilot for 'ground looping', a careless form of returning to earth. Bill Shattock protested, but the raving continued. The navigator shouted: 'Ignore the stupid sod!' The medical officer was by then pressing the crew to climb into the ambulance to go to collect another aircraft standing by. The navigator spied a tea truck and insisted on a cup and cigarette before they took off after a few minutes. Again they were berated for being late, and relegated to the last take-off at 03.10 hour, being effectively the dawn patrol on the night of the Salerno invasion.

The sequel was a 'Green Endorsement' for skilful airmanship in Bill Shattock's logbook by the offending senior officer. This infrequent 'commendation' was the perfect apology as the pilot was about to appeal to Air Vice Marshal Sir Keith Park against the unfair and unwarranted criticism.

At about the same time the injunction from above had been to 'Stop all night movement behind enemy lines. Bash their lines of communication close and far behind the bomb line.' This was interpreted in verbal exhortation as in 'If anything moves hit it with bombs, cannon or machine guns, or all three. If it is a pram, hope that twins are in it!' The last comment sickened many airmen, some of whose wives were pregnant and constantly in their minds.

The persistent drone of warning sirens hardly ceased over a vast swathe of Italy – night after night. The routine was to patrol an area, looking for activity at aerodromes, railway lines and stations, bridges and road convoys of vehicles (or even individual cars that might contain staff officers) from dusk to dawn. In England it might have been a region like Nottingham–Manchester–Leeds–Nottingham. Any sign of movement brought a rapid diving attack with a nightly cannonade. If the target merited, two 250 or 500lb bombs were added to the assault. After the period allotted – an hour or more, according to fuel position – a fresh crew relieved the patrol. Short messages were sometimes passed by Very High Frequency (VHF) radio, with cryptic indications of 'juicy targets'.

The technical problems of the pilots in getting airborne from indifferent bases, avoiding weather conditions and savage terrain, and searching out and attacking targets of opportunity, had to be overcome. The navigator had to indulge constantly in mental gymnastics of calculation, with minimum assistance from meteorological forecasting. At strikes he had to think (during brain-numbing crash and chatter of cannon and machine guns) of speed and direction, location, and above all safety heights. Speeds of 300mph were usually exceeded in a series of strafing attacks. The primary task of conveying safety heights to pilots who took little notice 'in the heat of the moment' was best done by physical blows on the arm or leg. Pilots were often mesmerised by targets, and pressed on in a suicidal way. The less aggressive they were on the ground, the more fearless and conscientious they were over enemy territory. The occasionally heard bravado on the ground was recognised for what it was.

The 'mush' effect as an aircraft continued to descend, despite changing to a climbing attitude, was an incalculable factor. Lagging and therefore inaccurate altimeters did not help. Many crews were undoubtedly lost by flying into the ground at unmarked heights, and hills were often seen above wingtip level in the moonlight, which gave false confidence.

Like swarms of hornets the aircraft buzzed around Luqa and Ta' Qali and nearby Hal Far. Gone were the days when a trio of Gloster Gladiators − 'Faith, Hope and Charity' − hopelessly waged a gallant defensive fight. Also, the months were long gone when Canadian pilot 'Screwball' Beurling and his mates clawed down the Luftwaffe and Regia Aeronautica as Malta was plastered to end resistance. Those Spitfires, flown from aircraft carriers, transformed the day air war over Malta. High scores and personal reputations were incidental to the maintenance of the island as a viable base.

Into this busy zone of operations came the rested Squadron Leader Murphy, eager to write some new pages in the history books.

Chapter Eight

Sticky's Mediterranean Service until May 1944

When the much-needed reinforcement of Squadron Leader Murphy landed in Malta, morale was poor. Aircraft and crews had been depleted by the end of the Sicilian campaign. Survivors felt they were regarded as expendable, as engine failures were frequent and although some crews reached base after long flights on one engine, others were lost. Warm night temperatures made overheating and engine failure likely. Great strain was placed on one glycol-cooled Merlin engine, whether Mk 21, 23 or 25, with operational loads of cannon and machine-gun ammunition and bombs, not to mention necessary fuel. UK performance of climbing and aerobatics on one engine was impossible. Frequently an engine burst into flames following low-level strafing attacks hundreds of miles from base, with high mountain ranges supervening. Only occasional survivors reported.

Others followed Sticky, including a veteran squadron crew from the Havoc and Boston days on No. 23 in the UK. They were Poles named Wladislaw Rosycki and Eduard Ryciak – flight lieutenants known as 'Rose and Ritzy'. The pilot (Rosy) had been aerobatic champion of the Polish Air Force in 1926, and was the exception to the rule, 'You can have an old pilot, and a bold pilot, but not an old, bold pilot.' He had little knowledge of English, just wanted to kill Germans, but both wore the Polish War Cross, with Rosy also wearing the Polish VC – the 'Virtuti Militari'. Ted Ryciak was more urbane, a friendly, always smiling man, who spoke English well, and proved a welcome addition to the mythical 'Navigators' Union'. Each survived the war and exceeded 100 sorties against the

Germans, but never lived again in their beloved Poland. They were reminders to younger members of the origins of the war in 1939.

In late September 1943, the 'heel' of Italy had fallen to the Allied advance. Airborne troops had landed from ships of the Royal Navy at Taranto. Quickly they cut across to Bari and Brindisi. The Eighth Army had crossed the Straits of Messina and were pressing up the mountainous sole of the Italian Front towards the heel and beyond. This meant that the 'bomb line' – showing areas that could be attacked – moved daily, but was found to be somewhat dubious.

A reduced number of sorties caused by shortage of aircraft, and the retreat northwards from Malta of the war, brought boredom and frustration to the nocturnal airmen, who often played Monopoly and cards all night, having lost the normal rhythm of life.

Those who took off at night from Sicilian landing grounds were called 'pipistrelli' (bats) by the peasants, who meant the furry-winged variety. Soaring over the rooftops and avoiding Mount Etna, about 11,000 feet high, in darkness and with dodgy compasses, needed care and concentration. Seeing the jagged and threatening mountain ranges of Sicily in daylight horrified crews who had plunged into the valleys, strafing and intruding over the same terrain for months, the moonlight concealing the now visible dangers.

Quickly sensing low morale, and recognising the cause of the NCO aircrews' reaction to his overture with bottles of wine, Sticky acted. He maintained the possibility of leave for all, away from the island. The squadron stood down from operations for a week from 25 October and Cairo was mentioned. However, leave did not materialise because the recently arrived squadron commander, Wing Commander Peter Burton-Gyles, DSO, DFC, had screwed from higher command early use of an airfield, Pomigliano d'Arco, on the Neapolitan plain, while shots were still being exchanged in Naples.

Before this, during the frustrating period, Sticky made several abortive trips to Sicily where Sigonella, a muddy airstrip, had become waterlogged at times. On 29 September 1943 Burton-Gyles cancelled operations for the night, and he and others had a party with Squadron Leader Murphy. After some local wine had been absorbed, he and Sticky solemnly played

78rpm records on a gramophone. They were hilarious when the needle stuck in a crack, but savagely devoured fried eggs in large quantities with their fingers.

From 2s 6d per egg on the Maltese black market, the abundance of eggs, fruit and wine in Sicily was a bonus not to be missed. When the Government froze the price of eggs at 1s 10d each, all eggs in Malta disappeared from the market. Now large baskets of eggs, oranges and lemons were put into RAF aircraft and flown to Malta. The black market collapsed. Wing Commander Burton-Gyles was a veteran airman and operational pilot, but seemed shy to his crews. Sticky's exuberance proved infectious and drew the CO out of his shell. They achieved a rapport that made for a happy squadron atmosphere. Burton-Gyles had arrived on 11 September 1943 – less than a fortnight before Sticky, who made his first local operational trip on 5 October.

It was the usual acclimatisation sortie in the Med, being a reconnaissance of the battle area. They flew at heights between 8,000 and 10,000 feet on a general look-see of the region south of Rome. Visibility was very poor, the moon was down early and of little assistance. Nothing more than a concentration of artillery fire was seen in a trip lasting three hours and fifty-five minutes.

On the afternoon of the next day, 6 October, Sergeant Bill Shattock, with Kit Cotter of the Royal New Zealand Air Force sitting on his navigator's feet, led a formation of Squadron Leaders Murphy and Rabone on a night-flying test to Gerbini Main from Luqa. Here they found a more solid short airstrip. Like playful puppies the two wingmen exchanged places several times, enjoying the daylight exercise and chance to illustrate and display their skills. Bad weather cancelled any opportunity of operations and brought a quick return flight to Malta.

On the evening of 10 October, Sticky again flew with Bilbe-Robinson on an offensive patrol to the roads south of Rome, bounded by Terracina, Cassino and Rome. Cannon attacks followed on three railway stations and various motor transport. Good weather and visibility helped.

Again from Gerbini Main after midnight on 20 October – but this time with his regular navigator Flying Officer Jock Reid, who had hitchhiked from England – Sticky operated north of Rome. During the period of patrol – 1.30–2.30am – a number of cannon attacks were made on various railway stations and road traffic. It was essential to adhere to patrol times to avoid fights between comrades in poor conditions of visibility.

Six aircraft of 'A' Flight, commanded by Squadron Leader Jock Brown, with his Canadian navigator, Flight Lieutenant Harry Waggett, beat up Sliema as they set off on 31 October for the new operational base of Pomigliano – quickly called 'Pommy' or 'Pomig'. This advanced field, close to the recently captured Naples and only about twenty-five miles behind the front line, was a great improvement from a distance point of view, but had operational disadvantages. There was an Alfa Romeo factory, in ruins, on the field and a solid but short landing strip. A series of power lines at one end could catch an aircraft landing or departing, and any easterly overshoot was fraught with danger. 'Foothills' of over 4,000 feet lurked nearby, together with Mount Vesuvius. Take-off with full loads of fuel, ammunition and bombs was hazardous, with turns having to be taken before safe speeds were possible. They were hair-raising experiences in the blackness of night.

On 4 November two crews flew back to Malta to exchange aircraft and bring news of conditions, which in addition to the flying difficulties included sleeping on the muddy field with flying clothing a must, digging slit trenches against enemy bombing attacks (which occurred), but brought a welcome change in the food, cigarette rations etc. now that the United States Fifth Army was producing supplies.

'B' Flight was anxious to get cracking, after the frustrating weeks in Malta, and set to with a vengeance on the night of 11 November 1943. Few backward glances had been given to Malta, the day flight over former occupied airspace proving fascinating. Like sparkling jewels, on a beautiful day, islands varied in bright blue and green hues. War, now so near, seemed an age away. It was a privileged day, still remembered. Lipari and the other Aeolian islands, north of Sicily, then Capri, Ischia and the volcano Stromboli, thrilled the eye. The glorious Bay of Naples gave no hint of the squalor and degradation of that city.

Sticky set the tone at once. He demonstrated the possibility of flying with bombs and full load off the strip, by day and night. 'If I get off OK, you chaps follow me.' That was leadership that was appreciated. At last the north of Italy was brought within range, including the industrial areas of Milan and Turin, and supply routes to both fronts.

Sticky and Jock led the way. That first night they flew a four-hour intruder sortie from 7pm to Ghedi and Villafranca, German-occupied aerodromes on the Lombardy Plain, and visiting Lakes Trasimeno and Garda for navigational checks. Finding the airfields non-operational they attacked two steam trains, as well as station buildings and motor vehicles.

The rest of 'B' Flight hunted, harried and hammered the enemy over an area including the route northwards to Rome and the Po Valley, from the Riviera dei Fiori in the west to the eastern communication route to Rimini and the Adriatic coast.

The enemy honoured and recognised the effectiveness of the attacks and paid a visit at first light as night fliers were asleep. About fifteen Focke-Wulf 190 fighters swept in low, without warning. Strafing and bombing with anti-personnel bombs, they concentrated strikes on the corner where the Mosquitoes were parked. Belatedly, trousers were split as airmen threw themselves from tents into nearby slit trenches, the medical officer almost strangling himself with his revolver lanyard.

It was a salutary lesson that attacks were a two-way traffic. No harm was done to RAF personnel, and only very minor damage to aircraft, but the German pilots must have thought they created havoc. It was a brave sally, and their riposte showed they were not finished, as had sometimes been suggested.

That same night the Mosquitoes struck again far and wide. Sticky and Jock took off later, and from 10pm flew for about four hours on an offensive patrol covering the area of Pavia–Allessandria–Genoa. Repeatedly they attacked three steam trains, and one driven by electricity, with such gusto that they ran out of ammunition. This was one tip the NCOs could have given them. At 9,000 feet Sticky and Jock saw a Junkers Ju 88 flying about 1,000 feet below over Lake Bolsena, but without ammunition to engage it only a lesson was learned.

At dawn American Spitfires were airborne, but no further attack came. They showed frustration by low and noisy passes over the tents of those trying to sleep with one ear open. Apart from the pilots, the twitchy British anti-aircraft gunners were alert for a second strike. Sleep was hopeless at Pomigliano d'Arco. Mosquitoes kept the others awake at night by their arrivals and departures. Several hundred other aircraft of the United States Army Air Force (USAAF) kept No. 23 Squadron night fliers awake by day.

A bumper crop of targets hit was reported by Mosquito crews for the two nights, including nineteen trains, railway stations, motor vehicles, searchlights and aerodromes. On the third night Sticky and Jock offensively patrolled the Lucca–Leghorn (Livorno)–Florence region, and at 9.33pm at 7,000 feet they received a visitor. A Messerschmitt 210 night fighter intercepted them in the moonlight, but was evaded despite apparent use of radar. Sticky later delivered two 250lb bombs at a railway station, having failed to jettison them in the excitement. He also strafed an electric train, exploding wagons, and had a go at motor transport. It was exhilarating to all to find plenty of targets, in the efforts to disrupt German supply columns.

Life was never dull, but it poured with rain all day on 14 November, making a quagmire of Pomigliano and no operations were tried. Some peace and sleep came to hundreds of thousands of people throughout Rome and northern Italy. Physical damage caused by the persistent Mosquitoes was nothing by comparison with the psychological harm that repeated nightly air-raid warnings caused. Robbed of sleep by warnings almost hourly, the population now had the automaton life that the British had experienced during late 1940 and parts of 1941.

But the respite was brief and on the 15th more sorties were carried out, in poor conditions, but flying to Milan and the Po Valley was a wonderful trip, with moonlit snowy mountains and the top of Mount Corno peeping through a fleecy blanket, giving a position line up the backbone of Italy. Overhead the stars blinked in the black velvet of the Mediterranean night sky. The Mosquito pilot had multiple switches in the dimly ultraviolet-lit cockpit, and his navigator, sitting as in a motor car, had more than twenty to care for at his right shoulder and memorise their functions. These included fuel gauges to be checked repeatedly when climbing to clear cloud at about 10,000 feet. The BBC reported that Mosquitoes had bombed cities in northern Italy after cloud was broken in a small hole, right over a flak-defended place that was rewarded with bombs. One Mosquito was damaged on landing in deep murk, having been fired at on the circuit on take-off and again when about to land by

nearby light anti-aircraft crews of the United States Army. The crew
was unhurt after taking a concrete mixer as a hurdle, but the aircraft
was unhappy at the loss of an undercarriage.

Heavy rain followed and rubber boots were obtained, but even
sleeping on makeshift beds in tents that had now been scrounged was
taken in the stride. Useful work was now being done, and Sticky led his
men on the crest of a wave. On the night of 16 November he and Jock flew
Mosquito 'L' to Venice and the Po Valley, finding cloud down to 300 feet
in the Venice area. They came down on the Adriatic coast and dropped
two 500lb bombs on a railway bridge twenty miles south-east of Ancona
before setting out for base in the early hours in bad weather. Others of
the flight bashed on in similar sorties, but one crew, Flight Sergeants
Bentley and Vic Causeway, were killed on one of their first few operations. They were so keen to get in on the scores of trains strafed, having
seen nothing before, that the tent on Pomigliano rang before they took
off with warnings to 'softly, softly catchee monkey'. Those who did not
operate that night had a premonition of their loss. They were buried in
the mountainous Communist republic of San Marino, south of Rimini,
and the local population provided a special monument to them.

Continuous rain followed for several days, but mischief was never far
away from No. 23's thoughts. Visits to Naples proved that it was 'a squalid
filthy hole full of beggars and brothels', as one contemporary diary shows.
One of the sex-starved airmen returned after disappearing for a few days.
He brought back black silk panties, French style and slightly torn, as a
trophy. Too tired to argue, he was relieved of his find and they became
'Sister Anna's Banner'. Suitably mounted on a wooden frame, the panties
took an honoured place in the bar, which for months afterwards rang
with the chant:

'Sister Anna, you carry the banner.
"I carried it last week." [sung in falsetto]
You carry it this week.
"But I'm in the family way."
You're in every bugger's way.'

Of such material was fun obtained, as spirits were released in hearty sing-songs in drunken booze-ups. Sticky now rendered his party piece, 'Rip My Knickers Away'. His willing but raucous tones echoed in the tents, and the card-playing light anti-aircraft crews invited to share the large cookhouse tent that doubled as mess and bar loved to hear the equivalent of a major proving that he could play as hard as he could fight. During this spell more Mosquitoes were collected from Malta and it became clear that 'B' Flight were bound soon for Sardinia, where operations to the Atlantic could be combined with the German aerodromes of Marseilles and northern Italy as targets.

At Pomigliano only a 30cwt truck was available as squadron transport, and this led to dependence on Americans for getting around – almost every USAAF crew had the ubiquitous Jeep, essential in the melted snow and rain. Of all the establishments in Naples, the Arizona Club was the most riotous. Here, western cowboy-style shootouts took place among the American troops resting from the Fifth Army front a few miles away. Fortunately they were usually too drunk to shoot straight, but No. 23 Squadron airmen tried to avoid testing this contention as their Sten-gun ammunition for Smith & Wesson .38 revolvers had to be filed on the rim to fit. Only about one bullet in five was therefore fired, although this was not to be relied on in any gunfight confrontation.

However, after one hectic party the Arizona Club provided temporary treasure. A Jeep, with keys still in the dashboard and a full tank, lingered outside. Two officers thought they would collect this for Sticky Murphy, the flight commander, whose dashing style was somewhat cramped by lack of transport. Painted black and bearing the legend in Brooklynese 'De Doity Twenty Toid' in white paint – following this comment from a New Yorker who thought it unfair to fight at night in filthy weather – the Jeep was presented to Sticky. He was delighted, and as a former scrambler he skidded around the aerodrome like a child with a new toy.

A few days later a provost marshal's deputy and staff arrived at one end of Pomigliano aerodrome. He had been tipped off by a thief who was in custody. Some measure of extrasensory perception appeared to be involved as the Jeep, hidden in a tent, was driven by the person responsible, and an aide, quickly out of the aerodrome in the opposite direction and abandoned near Pompeii. The chagrined searchers departed empty-handed.

A visit to Pompeii ruins previously brought back stories of clear evidence of a former town of 28,000 people with an arena to accommodate 20,000. Public baths, a market square, place of worship, law court, library and other social amenities were seen, apart from the notorious brothels with carved illustrations. The Pompeii red paintings were admired and, in view of the antiquity, it was a Philistine who said: 'Just fancy, Naples has always been one big brothel. It was not the war and starvation that did it.' The Italian guides were as pleased to show Allied servicemen around as they had been for the Germans.

Warnings were prevalent about Italian prostitutes being infected deliberately by the Germans with venereal disease, and German snipers still firing from rooftops in the congested backstreets. Flight Lieutenants Conquer and Bilbe-Robinson captured one German soldier, who claimed to be French, and then Arab. He could not speak in either language and wore a mixture of British and American uniforms. This was not unusual with Americans who liked the warmth and quality of British Army greatcoats. They also liked bully beef and British bread, and swaps for tinned fruit, chicken and spam were eagerly made.

During late November the United States of America's Thanksgiving Day was celebrated for the first time by No. 23 Squadron, with great gusto. Fifteen of the live turkeys that had been flown from America for this festival were allocated to the squadron, and guarded from marauding Italians. Shrunken stomachs from Malta days were overstretched joyously. That gnawing pain was still remembered, and one navigator who weighed under 140lb at six feet four inches tall was living proof. Two pilots were suffering from tuberculosis at this time from the months in Malta. One of them recorded about Balluta's sergeants' mess: 'The food we have I normally wouldn't give to a pig – in fact I've seen my grandfather give better food to his pigs.'

Shorty Dawson had soon lost his distaste for Sticky's style, and used to shake his head and say: 'Jeez, that Sticky's a cool geezer. He's always up to something. He never stays still.' Shorty's 'sangfroid' matched that of his flight commander, and this author recalls one example he shared.

Fergie Murray had returned to Malta alone, and a night-flying test in a Mosquito with Shorty took place over the Bay of Naples. Water in the petrol was causing concern and engine failures. At about 1,500 feet both engines cut and died, and the plane dropped smartly towards the sea. The coast was in sight, but impossible to reach without power. There was no known instance of a Mosquito surviving a ditching, despite the wooden construction in many parts, and parachuting was too late and of dubious wisdom as only navigators were thought likely to escape in that manner.

The unhelpful comment, 'We are going to get our feet wet, Shorty', was made as the pilot swore and pressed tits and pulled levers. Just as straps were tightened, feet braced and a door about to be jettisoned on impact, both engines fired and a splash was just avoided.

'Jeez, I thought I was going to spoil my new boots and get them wet,' said Shorty to a speechless navigator as they headed straight in for a land-ing. Even Shorty, who could swim like most local fish, had not fancied their chances of surviving a prang in the sea.

At this time the Polish crew lost 3,000 feet in a sudden drop in turbulence, seeing lights of villages above them as Rosy regained con-trol. 'Not a good fly out there,' he remarked when being debriefed.

Urgently the Germans tried to reinforce and supply their armies in the field. By day the Allied air forces struck relentlessly at bridges, junctions and lines of communications. At night the Mosquitoes harried and threatened all movement, strengthened by light and heavy bombers of the Tactical Air Force, as the Desert Air Force had been renamed since arriving in Italy. Despite some curtailment by atrocious weather during November 1943 that had brought ground forces almost to a halt, No. 23 Squadron expended 3,200 20mm cannon shells and fired 5,460 .303 machine-gun bullets and dropped 230 general-purpose bombs on a wide variety of targets.

On land the front advanced very slowly, terrain, weather and heavy resistance accounting for lack of speed. A forward thrust by French Colonial troops through the central mountain region was not anticipated by the Germans, who feared no activity there. Goums – Arabs from the Atlas Mountains – used pack mules and were familiar with this type of territory. They had been seen in Naples, like human wolves, revelling in the facilities. Now the Germans found them ingenious and formidable foes in high terrain.

Ablutions were minimal at Pomigliano, and the communal lavatory was a bucket with a seat in the middle of a grassy patch. As one of the more lustful members of the squadron sat communing there, reading the local Services paper, The Union Jack, he fell into a daydream. Failing to notice their gradual advance, he suddenly heard the black-clad peasant women as they surrounded him, cutting away at the grass for fodder with scythes. 'Buon giorno, Signore,' they greeted him as they discussed with him whether he had any laundry to be done. He was embarrassed for a short time, but was soon off on a foray to Naples – 'To do some shopping' as he put it. Starvation forced families to sell wives and daughters for food or cigarettes for trade. Many Servicemen gave soap, chocolate and cigarettes away without strings, thinking of their own families' shame if in similar straits.

At midday a Mosquito appeared over Pomigliano with a Spitfire in mock pursuit in a simulated dogfight. Hurling the Mossie about the sky, Sticky Murphy gave the American pilot a good scrap before an unorthodox landing. It had been too good a chance to miss with a single-engined fighter available. Sticky had flown the Spitfire and knew the handling characteristics. Me 109s and Focke-Wulf 190s were the main threat to Mosquitoes. The general opinion on No. 23 Squadron was that either German fighter needed a dive to catch a Mossie at full throttle. No first-hand reports were available in this theatre, although a Messerschmitt 210 had been downed in a dicey dogfight by Flight Sergeant Rudd from Malta in daylight, and Shorty had shot down a Dornier 217 after his Palermo one-engined landing and escape from death.

At this time six armed and hatless men strode purposefully into a department store in the commercial centre of Naples. Some wore leather flying jackets and others a miscellany of RAF blue battledress with khaki trousers, and American gear. All wore well-muddied flying boots and revolvers and were gaunt and dishevelled. As they entered there were shrieks from the female assistants. 'La RAF,' they cried, fleeing in all directions.

The men continued on, through various departments, searching eagerly and ignoring the customers and staff who appeared so frightened. Rape seemed the least of their intentions. Finally the aircrews reached their counter destination. The spokesman for the group delivered his demand in halting Italian: 'Avete gli anelli per I denti dei bambini, per favore?' ('Have you any babies' teething rings, please?') Cowering, the young girl assistants asked him to repeat what he had said. Broad smiles appeared through the tears of apprehension, and masses of teething rings were produced, as well as a great deal of baby paraphernalia. Making large purchases on their own behalf, and for comrades, the six departed. Many had new babies and others had events awaited daily. Embarkation leaves enabled Nature to replenish operational losses. It was not general knowledge that Sticky was one of the expectant fathers.

Clouds were almost literally on the ground, and a party in full swing, on the night of 3 December, when operations had been cancelled because of the weather. Urgent orders came from Tactical Air Force headquarters for any aircraft to be sent to intrude on Villafranca Aerodrome in the Po Valley at once. Germans had made a very successful bombing raid on Bari harbour on the east coast of Italy, above the 'heel'. Three Junkers Ju 88s based near Milan had used strips of aluminium foil (known as 'Window') in the RAF Bomber Command way, to fool the radar operating in defence of southern Italian ports. Villafranca was a forward base to assist range. Parachute mines, as well as bombs, were used and an early hit exploded an ammunition ship, which then set fire to neighbouring vessels. One rumour said that mustard gas was carried for defensive purposes. Over ten merchant ships caught fire, with a figure of 1,000 dead and injured estimated. Not surprisingly, in view of the weather conditions, no interceptions were made at the target.

Weather was not expected to improve at Pomigliano, and the solid clouds sitting over the surrounding mountains lurked nearby. Despite having absorbed much local wine, and being very merry, Sticky Murphy and Alec Lawson, with navigators, became airborne somehow, before 11am. Jovially they headed for Villafranca as ordered. Their fearful comrades held their collective breath as the Mosquitoes disappeared into the black clouds that hovered over the runways. 'They are too far gone to see how suicidal it is,' they said, expecting to hear explosions as their comrades perished nearby. Despite this both aircraft found Villafranca where there was no activity and cloud was down to 700 feet. On the way back, both crews strafed buildings and odd motor vehicles as opportunity occurred. They landed back on base to cheers, now very sober and chastened. The raid on Bari was one of the most successful of the German Air Force in the Mediterranean area.

A few days prior to this raid, an RAF film unit arrived at Pomigliano on public relations business. The cameraman had worked on recent propaganda features, and film and still photographs were taken of crews in wellington boots, with Burton-Gyles and Sticky Murphy. The photos appeared in UK papers with news of the aggressive Mosquito aircrews in Italy, in terms such as 'On Mosquitoes' wings these airmen, formerly serving in Malta GC, created recent havoc behind enemy lines.' This was all information censored from letters home. A war correspondent, Ronald Legge of *The Daily Telegraph*, wrote from 'Mediterranean Airfield':

This is the story of an extraordinary band of young men and an extraordinary plane. The men are members of an RAF squadron, based here, who style themselves facetiously, but with a touch of pride, the 'Independent Air Force'. They have also been likened to 'flying Micawbers' because of their indefatigable patience in waiting for 'something to turn up'.

The machines they fly are Mosquitoes, ultra-fast fighter-bombers best known in this theatre for their 'intruder' operations and in Britain for the sharp stings they give regularly to Berlin. But the Mosquitoes which fly from this airfield are pirate ships and their crews are counterparts of the seamen Drake, Raleigh and Hawkins.

Their exploits are in the tradition of 'singeing the beard of the King of Spain'. Given a roving commission to inflict as much damage as possible along the German supply routes into Italy, they range far at night selecting their own targets. 'Train-busting' is their speciality.

Engine drivers in charge of locomotives drawing consignments of food and petrol and arms for the Germans have come to dread them. Their swift unheralded pounces from the sky and blaze of cannon have left much of the enemy's limited Italian rolling-stock as salvage jobs for breakdown gangs, imposing maximum strain on the enemy's communication lines.

Damage inflicted is known to have been a serious embarrassment to the Germans.

The Mosquito squadron of which I am writing occupies a comparatively small corner of a large airfield here from which the majority of aircraft and crews operating are American.

I found the commanding officer, Squadron Leader A.M. Murphy and a group of his co-pilots with Army and Navy liaison officers, in a tent. Murphy, a tall spare young man with a fair straggling moustache, gave me a description of the marauding expeditions. Medal ribbons – DSO, DFC and the French Croix de Guerre – proclaimed him a seasoned airman.

He told me that the crews are composed of British, Australian, New Zealanders and Canadians.

'We've had to learn to be patient,' he continued, 'work entails a lot of stooging around waiting like flying Micawbers for something to turn up. We like trains best of all. Extensive sections of the Italian railway system are electrified and often bright flashes from the live rail are our signal. If it is a steam locomotive you generally see a white jet of steam in the moonlight or a red glow from the furnace. As the bulk of the train becomes visible, creeping along the line, we dive on to it and open up with both cannon and machine guns. The train does not stand a chance. When we first began train busting and shooting up motor vehicle columns, we took the Germans completely by surprise. We were able to swoop overhead strafing to our heart's content without interference. Recently congestion on railways and damage to transport has resulted in their being equipped with guns. But their flak does not trouble us much.'

Murphy said the squadron had only two losses in recent months. The chief danger to pilots was the mountainous nature of the country. Some nights he and his men range as far as the Po Valley. They then have to select targets quickly because of heavy fuel consumption.

The ubiquitous and versatile Mosquito also usually takes along a couple of bombs just for 'makeweight'. The airmen drop them on any handy military target they can be certain of hitting. This particular squadron sets out on its missions unbriefed beyond instructions given to each crew to patrol a certain area so that there will be no overlapping, and that the maximum coverage will be ensured 'backstage'

of the theatre where the opposing armies are engaged. It was a
brilliantly conceived idea which had already yielded high dividends.
As Kesselring's troops have been pushed steadily northwards by the
Eighth and Fifth Armies, both strategical and tactical bombers have
carried out a regular programme smashing bridges, marshalling yards
and other railway installations.

Regarding the Bari raid of 3 December 1943, Ronald Legge recalled
from Rhodesia in 1974 of his being in the vicinity, with a party of London
correspondents who had been told by Air Marshal Sir Arthur Coningham,
Air Officer Commanding (AOC) the Tactical Air Force, that 'the Luftwaffe
has been shot out of the sky and is a complete write-off'. Legge continued:

I do recall what a grand chap Sticky Murphy was. We were driving in
a motor coach along the coast road towards Bari when the skies were
lit by flares, and bombs began dropping into the sea nearby. The chap
next to me, fresh from London, was so impressed by what Coningham
had said that he watched with consuming interest what was going on,
and then turned to me and said: 'You certainly put on some pretty
realistic practice out here, don't you?' As the Germans hit an
ammunition ship that night, and created indescribable havoc among
the shipping moored in Bari harbour, his remarks and the incident
are my more indelible recollection of that night.

He added: 'It was the most devastating single success by the Luftwaffe
in the Mediterranean throughout the war.'
    At this time, Flight Lieutenant David Porter, formerly of the BBC,
joined the squadron with another pilot, Flight Lieutenant Turner. By the
end of 1943 the squadron had lost twenty-five crews in the year; almost
half the total of the war. Sticky and Jock revisited Villafranca in northern
Italy with two 500lb bombs on the night of 5 December, and Sticky
carried out his forty-sixth sortie, with Flight Lieutenant Bilbe-Robinson,
on the night of 10 December, leaving a note: 'My last sortie before moving
my flight from Pomigliano to Alghero. Used all my ammunition on a
ship in a harbour south of Ancona on the Adriatic coast.'
    Alghero Aerodrome on the north-west tip of Sardinia was no improve-

ment on Pomigliano, except for a great increase of range in operations. Grass surface and a 1,400-foot hill on the circuit, which became known as 'Murphy's Mount', made landing akin to an aircraft carrier. Nearby were mountains more rugged and threatening than in the Naples area. Malaria was rife, and other dangers threatened. 'A' Flight was full of warnings about an imminent attack from more than 300,000 fully armed Italian troops, including parachutists. Abandoned to their starving fate, this army had never surrendered, and the island had not been occupied. The position was rather uneasy, as no British or American soldiers had arrived, and only two squadrons were present. Aircraft had to be protected by aircrews, who carried sidearms at all times, and billets – four miles away at Fertilia, where a barrack block had been taken over – also had to be guarded.

Within two days, Wing Commander Peter Burton-Gyles and Pilot Officer Jack Layh, an Aussie navigator who had flown with Wing Commander John Selby the previous squadron commander, were lost on a sortie to the Milan area, and just south of that city. Warrant Officer Tony Sullivan had flown to the same location, following their patrol, and found 10/10ths cloud that allowed no breaks during a long search. He returned to say that he had no intention of diving through the cloud as he had only a few trips left to do, and had not lasted this long by trying to commit suicide. Nothing was ever heard of the CO, and correspondence with Jack Layh's brother Ron, in Australia in 1978, showed that nothing had been heard of him either, a situation that had not changed on a visit to Devon by Ron in 1980.

Within a few hours of their loss, Ron Layh flew in to see his brother for Christmas in a Wellington bomber, and was welcomed and absorbed quickly into the family atmosphere of No. 23 Squadron, as he remembered clearly. Sticky Murphy became wing commander after a visit to Algiers, where control was now allegedly exerted. Alec Lawson, a boyish veteran and top carouser became flight commander of 'B' Flight as a squadron leader and was popular. He was a wild man who flew just as recklessly, but with panache. Discipline was not his strong suit, but as senior flight lieutenant he was the obvious choice.

From time to time reinforcements arrived, and an individual or crew made an early impact if they survived the first five sorties. Flying

Officer Buddy Badley of the Royal New Zealand Air Force and his navigator, Sergeant Jimmy James, were one of these crews. They provided a contrast in personality and style. Buddy was a happy, relaxed, slim young chap of twenty, who had finished his operational training in England. Despite his junior status he had no inhibitions about suggesting special targets, or otherwise contributing, and Shorty Dawson, Kit Cotter and he were now the only Antipodean contingent. Buddy became a dashing and aggressive pilot, fearless and happy, while Jimmy James was a quiet person, providing that equilibrium and common sense that successful and surviving crews needed.

Other characters who made their mark were Flight Lieutenants 'Baron' Goldie, and Norman Conquer – who had become squadron navigation officer. Norman had spent a year in hospital as a result of a bad crash at an Operational Training Unit in a Blenheim Mk IV when his pilot and air gunner were both killed. Goldie, the pilot, resembled a medieval 'robber baron' – large, red-faced and bluff. He had been a flying instructor and was a super pilot – once force-landing a Mosquito at Alghero with no wheels, gently and with minimal damage. They were great party men, and enlivened what now became a hectic social scene when operations were over or cancelled.

Sticky was unchanged as commanding officer, leading in every way, and Christmas 1943 was most festive. Plenty of booze, of dubious quality, was obtained, and although trafficking with the local population for food was forbidden, forays in the truck were made into the mountains, suitably armed with goods for barter such as soap and cigarettes. Here contact was made with owners of sheep and goats and al fresco drunken picnics accompanied discussion by sign language of transactions. Pigs were trussed up and hidden in a roll-top tarpaulin, leaving the truck open. Such delicacies as goat kid, freshly slaughtered, were swallowed by the airmen, washed down with very rough red wine on open mountain sites.

The journeys back over bumpy tracks and roads around the gorges and ravines in Sardinia's hinterland were memorable. With chairs and tables in the truck, inebriated airmen played cards and sang in party spirit. A butcher and farmer on the squadron helped to ensure great care was taken with the Christmas fare, which, with American rations, assumed the proportions of a banquet.

The bar and other quarters had been furnished with chairs and additional furniture from the local prison at Alghero where it was made. An elaborate ritual of nonsense had to be gone through to get these goods, in exchange for cigarettes, sugar, soap and tins of meat. The prisoners were green with malnutrition – hardly surprising in view of the general situation on the island. Fergie Murray left behind him a trail of cigarettes and sweets, causing a minor riot.

Considerable hostility by the local population ceased to be open after Sticky Murphy had taken action to break the tension found in villages and towns. Bombing-up with wing bombs he led night-flying tests across and between chimneys in Sassari, off-duty crews hearing the full effect of the Mosquitoes as they walked in groups through that most hostile town. Suddenly smiles appeared and greetings from the local people, who had succumbed to the Murphy method of low-flying aircraft and visible bombs.

Douglas Higgins, the squadron artist, decorated with murals the mess at Fertilia, and on the night of 30 December, Air Vice Marshal Sir Hugh Pughe Lloyd, the AOC from Algiers, appeared for a party. Sticky suggested to John Irvin and this author that they keep an eye on any approaches made to the AOC when the wine had flowed, and they were not the only people to be rather abstemious. Sticky thanked them next day for plucking from the AOC's collar a disciplinary senior NCO who wanted to show his affection and esteem. However, this did not prevent the effervescent New Zealander, Kit Cotter, from telling the former AOC, Malta: 'You are not such a bad old bastard really!' The AOC had entered into the spirit and sang songs of the First World War, which only marginally differed from modern versions.

However, he upset the squadron, and put them on their mettle, when he departed after, stating: 'Intruding is finished in the Mediterranean.' He had urged special attention to be given to aerodromes in southern France, especially at Toulouse and the Istres group near Marseilles. This was somewhat contradictory, but shipping convoys along the North African coast had been attacked by aircraft from Spain or France. Many ships were full of time-expired men from the Eighth and former First Armies returning to England for the impending Second Front – the invasion from England or France, Belgium or Holland to finish the war.

Unlike many Mosquito crews, Sticky and Jock Reid did not socialise together. Sticky was for constant action, and Jock enjoyed a quieter life and preferred playing cards to drinking parties. Yet they were complementary. Sticky's enthusiasm was curbed by Jock's basic caution. Few others could apply the gentle brake to Sticky. In late 1974 Jock recalled:

On 5 January 1944 we flew our first operation from Alghero, over the Gulf of Lyons with a weather forecast of a northerly wind at 35 knots. It turned out to be more like 60 or 70 knots, and the windscreen was covered in salt from the sea. We made landfall somewhere near the Costa Brava, and when we reached Toulouse at the foot of the Pyrenees, we could not remove the salt and saw a German aircraft flying near the aerodrome at Toulouse Francazal and lost him.

We decided to go back there the next night and in the afternoon, with good weather, did a night-flying test and very low flying over Sassari which some of the other lads observed. This was my tenth trip. We took off early, 17.20 hours, and from over 100 miles away could see the Pyrenees. We crossed the French coast at last light, at 18.30 hours, and arrived at Toulouse at 19.05, finding the airfield lit up and a Hun with navigation lights showing. We gave chase and caught up with him too quickly. After a short burst we had to break away sharply to avoid a collision, and had seen no strikes. We came round again, and I saw him again and pointed him out to Sticky, but once more we lost sight of the aircraft. Then we found him again and closed nice and slowly, going very low – passing a church tower with four pairs of red lights on top. We came right up below him, 50 to 100 yards away, and just as we fired he broke violently away and the rear gunner started firing back. I tucked my head down as the tracer whipped past.

We followed him round all the way, giving him a five-second burst but saw no strikes as the deflection was so great. We closed again, travelling to the west of the airfield and delivered another attack – he again returned fire. I was a bit jittery about it. Once more we attacked – he still had his nav. lights – why, God knows – again we saw no strikes.

At this point I told Sticky that we must be almost out of ammunition. He muttered something about **** armourers. Again we

attacked from 40 to 100 yards, coming up from the port quarter, and
to our joy saw two strikes on the starboard wing root. He turned
slowly to port, went up on his nose and dived straight for the ground.
We saw him all the way down, and he hit the ground on a main road
south of the airfield. The explosion was a thing I shall never forget.
The large mushroom of yellow flame seemed to come up almost as
high as us at 500 feet.

We nipped smartly away to the south at 200 feet, one gun firing at
us from directly beneath us. Searchlights came on from the airfield
and we set course for home. The aircraft had been identified as a
Dornier 217.

Squadron Leader Alec Lawson, with Flying Officer 'Robbie' Robertson,
arrived shortly after and later reported:

We followed Wing Commander Murphy into the Toulouse area and saw
that the aerodrome at Francazal had its perimeter lights on. Then some
searchlights came on and lit up a twin-engined aircraft which was very
promptly shot down by light flak from the airfield defences, while we
remained interested spectators. We are claiming this for the squadron.

Five minutes later we saw two aircraft about 200 yards apart. We
closed to 150 yards and gave a short burst at the rear one, finishing the
attack at 50 yards. There was an explosion and a large cloud of flame
and smoke. Then we saw big pieces falling off the aircraft, which we
recognised as an He 111.

A steep turn to starboard to avoid the Heinkel and we saw it burning on the ground. Then we found ourselves behind the other aircraft,
throttled back and stalked it at 200 to 220 miles an hour, opening fire
at 200 yards and closing to 50 yards.

A puff of smoke and a flash came from the port engine, and the
tail unit caught fire. We saw it was a Junkers 88. It turned steeply to
starboard and then over on its back, diving as it did so. The fire
seemed to blow out as it dived. Then we had to turn away. The last
we saw of the 88, it was diving straight for the ground at 150 feet in
a slightly inverted position. It could not possibly have pulled out.
The Mosquito then set course for base, wearing a satisfied smile.

The rest of 'B' Flight that night hit ten trains and destroyed thirty motor vehicles on supply lines in Italy.

The chance to send the AOC a signal was accepted: 'Hoping this disproves your theory about intruders. Two enemy aircraft destroyed by Squadron Leader Lawson, one enemy aircraft by Wing Commander Murphy, one enemy aircraft destroyed by enemy ack-ack. All at Toulouse. Ten trains and thirty motor vehicles attacked. Prosperous New Year.'

Much later, in 1976, when trying to trace women agents of SOE who had been landed or picked up by Sticky in his Lysander, there was correspondence with such an agent who had been serving in the Toulouse area at the time of the successes. She said that she had been absent in early January 1944 but upon returning heard of the attacks and positive results at Francazal. Unfortunately she put this down to Latin or Midi exaggeration, and was interested to hear the facts.

Unexpected allies were found in Sardinia among the thousands wearing Italian uniforms. These were from a labour battalion from the Gorizia and Tolmino area of north-eastern Italy, which before 1918 formed part of the Austro-Hungarian Empire, but was annexed by Italy, creating another sore spot. Claiming to be Slavs and with a dignity and integrity that set them apart, these men were at the end of the Italian food supply system. Stewing grass and herbs in large cooking pots they were suffering from malnutrition and malaria. An orderly, but pitiful, 'gauntlet' was formed by queues of Italian airmen and the 'Slavs' who spoke German, Italian and Yugoslav. Outside the cookhouse they held tins for the slops of stew, coffee and rice pudding, which were eagerly consumed. Also Greek prisoners had been forced into labour battalions and were present.

Airmen who remembered the hunger in Malta found increasing opportunities to fill the tins of those they considered most worthy, and a squad of 'Slavs' became batmen and general domestic assistants. First they were rewarded with tobacco and such food as was possible, but when Wing Commander Murphy was approached he put them on the ration strength, and this enabled them to feed compatriots by a system of self-rationing. Again and again they proved their honesty. One had been a tailor in Belgium, and pidgin Italian and French allowed contact to be maintained. He carried out much-needed repairs and alterations to uniforms.

One particular giant, despite his deprivations, had a red beard and a most gentle and dignified demeanour and manners. Others confided that he had been a major landowner in his own district, but he was pleased to clean lavatories and wash clothes with cold water.

Sticky continued to lead by example, and personality. His lack of superior airs, imperturbable freedom from fear, concern for others, love of a party, and amazing stamina while working or playing, perplexed his crews, who had not met his style before.

Sticky and Jock carried out another intruder sortie on the night of 10 January 1944, this time to France for five hours, but with no further success.

Despite his leadership there were murmurings among the crews because of the number of engine failures on take-off or soon afterwards. Causes were discussed. This came to a head on 20 January at Alghero. Some aircrews standing on the control tower watched the other flight carrying out night-flying tests by taking off, checking instruments and radio, and then landing after about half an hour. As one Mosquito revved and accelerated a plume of black smoke emerged from a backfiring engine. The pilot, one of the most popular, pressed on as watchers cried, 'Cut the engines!' But he was committed to the take-off and fascinated observers saw the Mossie rise, then heard the engine cough, before the plane lazily fell into marshy ground beyond the runway, just short of the sea.

Flames and smoke shot high into the sky, with explosions, as full operational loads of fuel and ammunition were consumed. Clearly no survival was possible for the crew. As he ran down the stairs, Wing Commander Murphy shouted, 'Everyone airborne. Low-flying practice in pairs!' The tradition of 'get them off the ground quickly' following a fatal prang was instinctive.

While Sticky, Buddy Badley and the medical officer jumped into the Jeep and tore across the intervening ground to what was now a funeral pyre, other crews scattered in pairs to grab a plane and obey orders. They took off hurriedly, as if in salute, rising through the pall of smoke, and scraping roofs of town- and farmhouses in a furious concentration of effort to ease the shock and pain. Another child was never to see its father. The pilot had been involved in the court martial of the Pomigliano thief, and thereby had lost much flying practice.

Positive action was then taken and the source of the petrol supply proved to be from open standing drums at Naples quayside, which had accumulated dew and rainfall before fuel was pumped from tankers, making a lethal combination that should have won someone an Iron Cross for assisting the enemy. Taking off each night into the blackness had been a nerve-tingling sensation with adrenalin pumping, imagination working, and ears listening for the slightest cough from the straining engines producing such power.

Operations continued with support to the Anzio landings by strafing and bombing the supply lines around Rome, and to the north of that city Sticky and Jock flew on the night of 23 January 1944. Although some intruders were carried out over French and north Italian aerodromes, much effort was then directed to assisting in the attempts to capture Rome. Tactical help was needed as much as ever.

Early in February Sticky and Jock flew to a target on the Atlantic coast – Bordeaux. Nearer to England than Sardinia, the lads had it worked out that any engine trouble would force them to fly to Cornwall. Trains near Bordeaux had been strafed by Flight Sergeant Griffiths and Warrant Officer Eric Maud on a pioneer flight to that target, but all Sticky got was a hole in his trousers from sitting for five hours and twenty minutes.

Some success had been achieved in southern France where the Istres group of airfields near Marseilles had been active. In poor weather conditions, and with indifferent visibility approaching base, crews generally preferred to fly under the low black clouds a few hundred feet high, from France to Sardinia. All navigation was based on deduced (dead) reckoning involving mental arithmetic. Windscreens were often thickly coated with salt from stormy seas. The mistral from the Rhône Valley blew aircraft at over 100mph towards Spain. Altimeter readings were governed by barometric pressure that misled in unsettled weather environments. This was another gamble, flying on dirty, dark nights, but with a gale blowing and turbulent conditions; it was all a risk, with the mountainous Sardinian coastline waiting, and Murphy's Mount on the circuit. One radar-directed crew was told they were over the sea, when lights of villages were visible above them in a valley.

Hearing a rumour that Sticky was flying to England to be briefed, this author made formal request to see him. It was too simple to tackle him in the mess on this subject. Having conjured up a cap and tie from somewhere, and remembering how to salute, an application was made to fly with him to England, operating to Bordeaux or elsewhere, in each direction. Lack of news of an expected child was the reason for the appeal, granted after Sticky had consulted his regular navigator Jock Reid. Regrettably, the Anzio landings caused the trip to be cancelled.

Squadron Leader Harold Lisson of No. 418 Royal Canadian Air Force (RCAF) arrived on a special mission (rumoured to be dropping gold bullion) to Toulouse resistance forces. Shorty and his mates were thrilled to see Harold, who had trained with them, and had to make two shots at his delivery. Apart from the pleasure of seeing a former friend and comrade still to be alive, he was a source, not only of home conditions, but also of information of present operations of the intruder squadrons. Operation Ranger was a daytime sortie in pairs of Mosquitoes, concentrating on shooting down all types of enemy aircraft, as well as strafing fighter, bomber and transport targets of all types. Harold explained how successful this had been with Squadron Leader Charlie Scherf of the Royal Australian Air Force – one of Shorty's old mates – becoming an 'ace' with a high score of aircraft destroyed. Rested, Scherf went to Intruder Control, but continued to operate on his 'days off' and knocked down more Germans.

To hear that their 'junior' intruder squadrons, Nos 418 and 605, were getting such success and freedom in daylight made No. 23 crews green with envy. Only rumours of Operation Ranger had previously come, but now concentrated practice day flights at low level in pairs was the order of the day. This was in complete contrast to the solo night intruder and offensive patrols where the difficulties of night vision and navigation were paramount. The low field of vision and greater impression of speed needed practice and care, but gave new life to squadron efforts. Meanwhile, night sorties continued. Sticky led immediate practice flights down mountain valleys, across coasts and simulated operations to France were repeated. That was where the Huns were to be found.

Fear, danger and death were never discussed, but most crews had become heavy smokers and drinkers. 'Round the bend' was another description of 'The Twitch', which might be defined as a state of extreme (if hidden) anxiety induced by persistent exposure to such perils as death or mutilation and the family consequences of such an event. It was obvious to others when the goal of a completed tour of operations came into view. Intelligence and imagination were enemies of aircrews. Enough sorties would break the nerves of men, however strong and brave. 'Depressed euphoria' was another definition, but the manifestation varied with individuals. It was a brutal act repeatedly to throw oneself into the furnace of operational flying, so often a cocktail of tedium, excitement and physical and cerebral activity. Frequently a physical tick or twitch of eye or face betrayed the condition. At other times a harmless or whimsical preoccupation with objects of obsession, either real or imaginary, occurred, such as a small dog or kitten fed and talked to. Comrades smiled tolerantly, unsure how serious it all was, and wondering what sort of twitch might be their reward for surviving sufficient sorties.

One real object of obsession was the boasted about massive male 'appendage' of another airman. He talked to it with promises of joy in Naples, and in Sardinia claimed that a German member of the local brothel demanded his social call before commencing her day's labour. That establishment was 'official', and many stories of constant queues, and of women puffing fag-ends from behind their ears between clients, came back to the squadron. Strangely enough, the longer airmen had been frustrated and starved in Malta (of sex as well as food), the less they were inclined to risk infection, and the squadron suffered little in that way.

The Squadron Diary recalls in January 1944 that someone had stolen Sticky Murphy's American hat that he wore when driving his Jeep – another 'De Doity Twenty Toid' – and this disappearance was greeted with glee by many.

The 'squadron linguist' eased his twitch by adopting the cause of the many slave labour Slavs, securing mepacrine from the medical officer for their malaria – rife in that area – and translating their duties as ancillary staff for the squadron, in an effort to ease their starvation and distress. One of Tito's generals came to recruit them, saying, 'Come and die as men with us, instead of rotting with malaria in Italian uniforms.' A BBC executive, David Porter, after a period of instructing as a pilot, joined No. 23 Squadron in Sardinia and made several sorties with his navigator, but was shot down in January 1944. Remarkably David survived and recalled in 1974 the events that ended his operational career:

Flying on operations from Alghero with my navigator I was in the area of Parma in the Po Valley of northern Italy. We made a diving attack on a train, which I missed, and almost immediately there was an explosion and my plane disintegrated. Somehow my parachute harness was released and I found myself floating down in the darkness, and saw the explosion and flames as the aircraft hit the ground some distance away below me.

When I landed on a sloping bank of a tributary of the River Po, this helped break my fall, but I was in great pain. My left arm had been completely dislocated from the shoulder and was useless and in rather an extraordinary position well below my shoulder. With my other hand, I put the left hand in my pocket after releasing my parachute, removing my badges of rank and rolling up the parachute with one hand and hiding it.

First of all I hid in some stacks of wood but found this uncomfortable because my arm was agonising. I therefore searched elsewhere and found that I could get under the top of the bank of the river where I hid. I heard Germans searching for me, apparently in some sort of extended line order. I was partly educated in Germany so that I could understand what they were saying, and it appeared that they had found a body in the aircraft (obviously my navigator) and were searching for two other men. I waited until they had passed and dirtied my uniform with earth and grass to try to look like a workman, and walked in the direction from which they had come. Finally I found a small farm and spent the night on the floor in an outbuilding. The next morning I saw the farmer and his wife and son and said the word 'Dottore' to them, indicating that I needed medical aid.

On the wife's bicycle, and accompanied by the farmer and his son, I went to the nearby village where they handed me over to the German Army. Not from what he said but from what I understood the Germans to be saying (and I still concealed my knowledge of that language) the farmer had asked them for 400 lire reward, which was promised by the Germans for anyone handing over escaped prisoners.

I do not know if he got the reward but I was attended to by an

Italian doctor who said to me 'Courage' (pronounced in the French way) and proceeded to jerk my arm, which did it no good at all.

Finally I was handed over to officers of the Luftwaffe, who treated me well and took me to Piacenza Civilian Prison. There a German soldier immediately knocked me to the ground and started to kick me. One of the Luftwaffe officers shouted at him and told him that I was a Hauptmann (as I had given my name, rank and number in accordance with orders) and shown them my badges of rank which I had put in my pocket.

The man immediately stopped knocking me about and sprang to attention and invited me to precede him into the prison. There was no more violence but I was subjected to solitary confinement and a German doctor set my arm under anaesthetic. He explained in perfect English, and with a sense of humour, that I had no doubt heard of the atrocities committed by the Germans, but I need not fear that he was going to do anything but fix my arm. He did so, and apart from my left arm being slightly weaker than my right, I have had no subsequent trouble with it.

I was then taken to Dulag Luft in Germany and finally to a prisoner of war camp, from which I was released in May 1945, eventually returning to the squadron at Little Snoring later that year.

I there had a flight in a training aircraft to acclimatise me.

I lost my father in the First World War, and Wing Commander Sticky Murphy, who had exchanged letters with my mother after my loss, was particularly sympathetic to her and included in his second letter to my mother, 'Blast the Hun', adding, 'he has a lot to answer for.'

Until mid-February 1944 there was a constant threat of attack by the Italians on Sardinia, but then more squadrons poured in, both American and English, followed by a French Walrus air-sea rescue squadron, which once operated at night to the amusing directions in French of torch-bearers, saying: 'Up a bit, down a bit.' The pilots had poor visibility and were unused to night flying. Sticky went to a party with the French and returned late at night with pockets full of names and addresses in France where aid would be forthcoming on any crashes. He solemnly destroyed these before his crews, indicating his comparatively sober state, saying:

'We could not fly with those names on us. The Germans would shoot them.'

Alghero Aerodrome was a mudbath. The Americans were applying their technical expertise to build a solid runway in one direction, but the wind seldom blew in a regular flow from the sea, or elsewhere, and was often fluky, and then at right angles to the chosen angle. During construction flying stones damaged the tailplanes of three Mosquitoes during night-flying tests.

At this period the United States Army Air Force were having a miserable time of it. They had P-39s – Bell Airacobras with 40mm cannon firing through the propeller boss, and engines behind the pilot. Propaganda had praised their performance as over 400mph, but pilots confided that this was nonsense, unless in a vertical dive, which was very likely to be the result of any sort of moderate aerobatics. They had been relegated to the ship-busting role off the French coast, and this was considered degradation for fighter pilots. One sortie too close produced a severe mauling from German Focke-Wulf 190s.

Therefore, the USAAF decided to throw a party, and officers and warrant officers of RAF squadrons were invited. They had visited No. 23 Squadron to see in the New Year, and wanted to show their own style. Euphemistically, a young officer's diary records for home consumption that, 'By special invitation we went to the American fighter squadron's mess for a party. It was one of the finest parties I have been to for a long time. Quite a lot of local girls turned up and we danced until two in the morning to a radiogram. There was a large variety of drinks, and very few were completely sober at the end of the evening. I was only very little the worse for wear and so refused to drive home with the types who had trucks there. The Yank Doc very kindly lent me his Jeep to get to our billcts.'

This account hid the story of what became known as 'The Orgy'. Lashings of food, booze and 'broads' (as the Americans insisted on calling the contents of all the brothels on the island) turned up, transported by the US Servicemen, with food being the greatest bait. A dangerous concoction called a fruit cup was prepared, with mixed wine and spirits, to which was added the final dynamite – namely pure medicinal alcohol! A wine glass proved too much for some, but one Italian blonde, of statuesque 'Sophia Loren'-like proportions announced, via one of the Italian-speaking American airmen, that she would drink anyone else under the table.

A large glass of the firewater was downed by her at a gulp, and soon afterwards another. Then followed a memorable dance solo during which she stripped completely with considerable style, and knocked back a third glass. That did the trick. She passed out like a falling tree, leaving her erotically aroused audience speechless. Quickly recovering, several ran to her aid and transported her upstairs to regain her equilibrium, while the party continued. The uninhibited atmosphere turned into a near riot, with the ladies' escorts at their wits' ends as they became increasingly unnecessary.

Finally, a lively No. 23 Squadron strongman had borrowed enough from others 'to buy that blonde for life' – as he insisted he wanted to do with the now-recomposed blonde stripper. Sabine style, he hoisted her over one shoulder and was on the way upstairs to the operational rooms when others grabbed him. Relieved of the blonde, and their own money, he was separated from his fancy by persuasive force.

The final scene of the night caused one navigator, recently arrived, to faint at the sight of a comrade who emerged from the mess. His best-pressed uniform had been smothered with tomato ketchup, giving him a bloody appearance. The fainter was driven home, and fortunately the bespattered officer had a sense of humour.

Next morning, to add to the hangovers, surreptitiously taken photo-graphs of the previous night's operations at the orgy, provided a somewhat pornographic spectacle in the operational tent. Some were delighted, but others made a frantic search for the photographer and negatives. No ill effects remained once heads had cleared, and it was described generally as 'a pretty good show'.

Daytime low-level practice continued in pairs, pending the required permission to take part in Operation Ranger. Sticky and Jock jumped the gun by a daylight reconnaissance alone to the Balearic Islands at low level, in case the Spaniards were sheltering German U-boats and/or aircraft. They had an interesting flight, found a submarine, and reported in great detail on the features of the neutral islands. They announced that Majorca and Minorca bore some resemblance to Sardinia, but were much smaller and less mountainous.

When intruding to the Atlantic Coast Flight, Sergeant Kit Cotter and his navigator, Flying Officer Al Yates, hit the jackpot. In twilight they found themselves near Montpellier on the coast of southern France, presented with five Heinkel He 111s in close formation, coming home to Marseilles. Kit shot one down immediately, but in his excitement overshot the others and lost contact in the poor light. He did tight turns over the downed Hun, muttering, 'Poor bastards.' Alec Yates took another view and laughed heartily. He thought they should have had three at least.

The same night Flying Officer Pat Rapson and Flight Sergeant Frankie White, a veteran crew by now – another great contrast in style – bagged a Hun near Marseilles. Five crews of 'B' Flight went to the Po Valley, but finding poor visibility and weather they strafed and harassed whatever they could find moving in the murk. Two nights later twelve aircraft returned to the Po Valley and ten trains were bashed, transformers attacked and much motor transport strafed, again by 'B' Flight, accompanied this time by Sticky and Jock.

Word came from enemy sources that Bentley and Causeway had died at San Marino, but usually crews vanished into the night with fate unknown, unless like Pat Rapson and Frankie White they force-landed elsewhere and subsequently found their way back to Sardinia. This sort of thing had happened several times. One crew, scrambled because they were most sober on a cancelled operations night, must have 'flown a reciprocal' as they finished up in North Africa instead of Italy. When they returned to base next day Sticky's only comment was, 'Have you got a girlfriend down there?'

He had a session that proved hilarious with the CO of No. 39 Squadron, and as this progressed for two days the adjutant of the other squadron appeared in the bar with a carpet as a drapery, saying that he had never felt like a bride before.

Squadron Leader Phil Russell, DFC, and his navigator, Flight Lieutenant Bill Gregory, DFC, veterans of the earliest No. 23 Squadron days in Malta, returned to the fold. Respectively they became flight commander of 'B' Flight and squadron navigation officer. The flight commander soon decided that there was too much drinking going on when off-duty, but Sticky could hardly reprimand the others and took the same view as Air Marshal Sir Arthur Harris concerning the therapeutic value of letting off steam in this way. 'Rusty', as he was known, soon left for

Egypt and suffered an attack of jaundice. He had found the atmosphere different from that under the leadership of Wing Commander Peter Wykeham-Barnes, DSO, DFC, who had been his passenger on a flight to England in the spring of 1943 – almost a disastrous trip.

The squadron intelligence officer, Flying Officer Ted Lewis, was a born courtier and a diligent worker to keep order out of chaos from reports of crews. Promoted to flight lieutenant he celebrated his promotion with the tour expiry of Squadron Leader Jock Brown and his navigator, Flight Lieutenant Harry Waggett, RCAF. Also from 'A' Flight, Warrant Officer Wally Morgan and Flight Sergeant Piggott had done their duty and were going home. DFCs were awarded to Brown and Waggett, who were debagged as was customary. Jock also found his cap full of crème de menthe, but could not have cared less by this time.

Work and play continued. Two Beaufighters came to try their hand but were lost the first night, flying into the neighbouring mountains without delay. The squadron's operational efforts were suspended on one day of gale-force wind and rain, and an interesting but disturbing visit took place.

Wing headquarters had arrived, as they called themselves, and caused aggravation by their demands for offices and other accommodation for chairborne gentlemen. These were places that Ted Lewis had fought to make presentable, and while Sticky was too polite to make loud noises that his crew could hear, he made it clear that he was not pleased. While visiting the new neighbours he met a naval officer escorting two members of the women's First Aid Nursing Yeomanry (FANY) on a visit. As Englishwomen were rare and delicate gems in that part of the theatre, he quickly accompanied them away and to the No. 23 Squadron mess where they were entertained. The senior Serviceman stuck to his guns and prevented any serious consequences, but some crews were mesmerised and incoherent, while others were upset by the impact of the two young women, who in turn were delighted by so much attention. As the Squadron Diary records: 'Sister Anna's banner [the pair of black French knickers brought back to camp from a Neapolitan sortie] moved gently in the breeze, caused by the subdued chatter on one particular subject. It seemed as if the sacred emblem had hopes of company on its lonely perch, but these hopes were thwarted by the eagle eye of the Senior Service.'

Sticky's final comment was, 'I only brought them down for you chaps!'

A more typical party in the bar grew from a few early arrivals who were not to fly that night. A few glasses of vermouth at the equivalent of three pence per glass warmed things up, until some was spilled on a concrete floor and by next morning had eaten into it. Then different new raw wines took over. Later, early flying crews and others arrived and invariably a sing-song happened, with 'We're a Shower of Bastards' – the squadron song – and further ditties, now well remembered. On one occasion a member of the Royal Navy motor torpedo crews from Maddalena, in the furthest north-west of the island, was brought in. His songs were almost identical, except for a salty flavour and amendment. They had a similar job of hit and run just off the Italian coast, and like No. 23, nights had become their days.

Some more lucky tour-expired airmen returned to England, including Shorty Dawson and Fergie Murray, John Irvin (his pilot George Twitt being stricken with tuberculosis), Alec Lawson and 'Robbie' from 'B' Flight, and Flight Lieutenant John Tracey and navigator Frank Beresford, as well as Hinchliffe and Bill Barclay, a rare Geordie, from 'A' Flight. All had been in Malta for the Sicilian campaign and were lucky survivors, with 'shaky dos' galore between them.

On 14 March 1944 an interesting flying night occurred for No. 23 Squadron, while 'B' Flight was operating and Sticky had popped over to Algiers with Group Captain MacDonald, the station commander, for an air force Ball. It was a wild night for flying, with low, black clouds and the mistral that funnelled down the Rhône Valley from Lyons playing havoc with navigation as far down as the Spanish border. Norman Conquer and Goldie went to Toulouse and almost hit the Pyrenees on the way home because at 9,000 feet the wind was in the 75mph region. Back at base a series of mishaps took place. Barometric pressure change was blamed for two crashes during which Mosquitoes were written off. First Kit Cotter made a good landing, despite the conditions and having lost one engine. Then Pat Rapson flew straight into the deck and splattered the Mosquito over the runway – fortunately without injury to Frankie White or to himself. Finally, the crosswind strip having to be used, and a few oily goosenecks being lit as the only aids, Bill Shattock flew directly into the ground, well short of the runway, his windscreen being heavily smeared with salt from a long and low crossing of the Mediterranean. This was his fourth bad prang, the others being much more praiseworthy. The Mossie was a series of bits and pieces.

Soon afterwards, Flying Officer Grimwood shot down the eighth Hun for the squadron since arriving at Alghero, a Junkers Ju 88, but within a few days both he and Flight Lieutenant 'Popcorn' Turner were lost in separate operations.

The odd sortie to the mountains for more bartering with the shepherds took place, and the use of small dugouts for picnics, as well as the Fertilia barrage. This involved shooting .303 rifles with tracer machine-gun ammunition at flocks of birds, which were never hit. However, when Wing went too far they were subjected to the barrage one night, and nothing was said about it. It had something to do with not inviting No. 23 Squadron to a reception for the ENSA (Entertainments National Service Association) party, which included actress Florence Desmond and classical pianist Kay Cavendish. After strafing the vicinity of the tent with tracer bullets the lads gave that up and attended anyway, queueing up to kiss the two ladies goodnight at the end of the festivities. Often feeling very expendable meant that crews appreciated anyone from home, and they all looked gorgeous after the swarthy local talent.

In early April a full-scale operation was carried out to block off the German retreat and supply columns around Rome in support of the Anzio landings. This was from dusk to dawn and some trains, and much motor transport, were claimed in a real old-fashioned Pomigliano-style bash.

Two days later a Ranger took place. It was Easter Sunday, and Sticky and Jock led Squadron Leader Smith, while 'Rusty' and Bill led Buddy Badley and Jimmy James. Cloud cover was supposed to be essential, to stand a chance, but on approaching the Camargue area at the mouth of the River Rhône, blue skies beckoned ahead.

As Jock said later: 'Undismayed, at least Sticky was, we flew south-west along the coast and went in about ten miles south of Montpellier where Sticky attacked a train, from which the driver seemed to have departed smartly. We then set fire to the gasholder at Sète, and seemed to run out of legitimate targets.'

Buddy became separated from Phil Russell and pressed on to the Spanish border at Perpignan, where he strafed the aerodrome, destroying one Dornier 217 and damaging two others before turning his attention to a train. All agreed that it seemed somewhat strange operating over enemy territory in daylight, but was exciting and well worthwhile in the hope of finding German aircraft, flying or otherwise.

Sticky and Jock carried out five more sorties into early May 1944, chiefly against military traffic in Italy, and also on another Ranger trip to southern France. Johnny Curd, former 'catafighter', accompanied them.

By now rumours were rife about the Second Front being launched from England, and the lads felt out of it, but on 4 May Sticky told the squadron that they would be returning home at once. At the same time, word was received that David Porter was a prisoner of war in Germany.

Football matches were now played, including one where Al Yates and Ted Lewis consumed all the booze laid on for halftime, and were hilarious. Other fun occurred when baling-out practice involved diving out of grounded aircraft on to tarpaulin sheets to break the fall. Sticky missed the target and knocked himself unconscious, considered great stuff by his fellow airmen. After recovery Sticky ruefully joined in the laughter.

A supply of alcohol was obtained from Naples and invitations sent out for a farewell party. No less than sixty bottles of spirits were knocked back, plus Sardinian and Italian liquor, which made packing next day somewhat hard. 'A' and 'B' Flights became airborne on 8 May and flew to Blida in North Africa, leaving the ground crews to follow by sea the following day in the Italian ship *Garibaldi* headed for Naples. There George Twitt joined them from hospital, still hoping to fly with the squadron once more.

Some 34,770 rounds of 20mm cannon ammunition, plus 36,030 .303 machine-gun rounds and 108 250lb bombs had been used operationally by No. 23 Squadron during April 1944. The Squadron Diary records:

In Algiers waiting for the boat to leave during May, naturally a lot of blacks were put up. Although the first day we arrived the CO asked the squadron to behave, the finest black was put up by the CO. After a party with Group Captain Vickers they returned to the Hotel Albert very full of liquor indeed, and proceeded to throw bottles from their bedroom windows at the gendarmes outside in the street. Of course they took a certain amount of umbrage, and the CO nearly found himself in Algiers Prison – which would have been very funny indeed.

On 15 May Sticky flew off to Casablanca in French Morocco to board a USAAF Liberator to return home. Engine failure forced a retreat to base, and a further flight on 18 May brought a safe landing in Cornwall at St Mawgan.

The troopship *Strathnaver* collected the whole squadron from Algiers on 20 May and the cry went up, 'Blighty here we come!' Spirits were kept up by refilling gin bottles with water after use, pretending an inexhaustible supply. Natural relief at going home, and a happy atmosphere fooled the baffled soldiers into thinking that liquor lasted the whole trip. Some 8 officers, 2 warrant officers and 23 senior NCOs, with 250 other ranks, finally arrived at the Port of Liverpool. Here they were met by Wing Commander Murphy, who had passed a few days with his wife Jean and new-born daughter Gail, before flying to West Raynham in Norfolk. Nearby he found Little Snoring Aerodrome close to Fakenham. The quaint name amused him, and he again met Group Captain Sammy Hoare, DSO, DFC, who was delighted to have 'his' old squadron coming under Sticky's command.

At Liverpool Sticky made two announcements to his crews. Firstly that he was the father of a baby girl, and secondly that Little Snoring was to be their new home base. Hearty congratulations given on the first statement and gusts of laughter on the second brought an adjournment to the nearest pub to celebrate in squadron tradition. Blighty had not changed Murphy's style.

Chapter Nine

Commanding No. 23 Squadron at Little Snoring, Norfolk – Bomber Support Squadron

At Little Snoring in Norfolk the North Sea was useful for navigational purposes if no fog occurred. Low-level approaches to the coast made memories fade of Sardinian mountains and 'Murphy's Mount' on the circuit at Alghero. Close by was Horatio, Admiral Lord Nelson's birthplace, and the area swarmed with squadrons full of his fighting spirit. Group Captain George Heycock, twice formerly No. 23 Squadron's commanding officer, was station commander at West Raynham Aerodrome, almost on Little Snoring's circuit.

On 14 June 1944 (a week and a day after the D-Day invasion of France), No. 23 Squadron crews mustered at their new base. Stories of family reunions were exchanged – Sticky Murphy being delighted to see his wife Jean once more, and thrilled with baby daughter Gail. His tales of nappy-washing and other domestic chores amused the lads, and the Squadron Diary records: 'What's it like to be a Daddy, Sir?'

The squadron replaced No. 169 Squadron at Little Snoring, and No. 515 Bomber Support Squadron of Mosquitoes shared the aerodrome. 'The Five-hundred and Fifteenth' (as Sticky called them) had by now recovered a high morale and state of efficiency after serious vicissitudes. In late 1943 they had arrived with single-engined Boulton Paul Defiants, an obsolescent fighter with a four-gun turret behind the pilot. Defiant crews had successively suffered bloody noses as day and night fighters, and by now were limited to special scientific night sorties to confuse enemy radar defences.

Re-equipped with Mosquitoes (a much more difficult aircraft to fly) and without undertaking a proper Operational Training Unit intruding course of instruction at High Ercall, casualties were inevitable.

In later January 1944 Wing Commander Freddy Lambert (a contemporary of Sammy Hoare and Canadian by origin) arrived to command No. 515. Soon Mosquito Mk II fighters turned up for conversion, and in March the commanding officer and other pilots, with their new navigators, went to Bradwell Bay where No. 605 Squadron blooded them in mock low-level attacks and intruder harassment. The host squadron had a long history of intruding, second only to No. 23 in time.

The arrival in March, too, of Squadron Leader Micky Martin, DSO, DFC, and Squadron Leader Paul Rabone, DFC – Sticky's predecessor as 'B' Flight commander on No. 23 in Malta – added weight and experience to the veteran Freddy Lambert's leadership. Martin was a gamekeeper turned poacher. He was the legendary Dambuster who had been described by Group Captain Leonard Cheshire, VC, DSO, DFC, as 'the greatest operational pilot the RAF had ever produced.' Grounded for a rest from operational flying, the Aussie Martin was posted to the newly formed No. 100 Group of Bomber Command. He lost little time in attaching himself to No. 515 Squadron. Who better than Martin to guard the Lancaster bomber stream? A great party man, he was pleased to welcome Sticky Murphy, whom he had met in Sardinia early in 1944. Mick's bomb aimer had been mortally wounded on the Antheor Viaduct raid in southern France, and medically qualified facilities were urgently needed. He had a high opinion of Sticky Murphy, and what he described as 'his gay and positive style of determined leadership'.

Freddy Lambert was a strict disciplinarian with a quiet personality, which contrasted with Sticky's, and No. 515 reflected his dedication and persistence. They also differed in regard to the wilder conduct of No. 23 Squadron, who still behaved as though they were in the Middle East – much to Sammy Hoare's regret. 'Cordite' was Lambert's nickname, but whether this was the short fuse on his temper, or because he had reported smelling the cordite of bombs he had dropped, was uncertain. At any rate he was very much in the thick of the action himself, and under his jurisdiction efficiency increased and the rate of casualties decreased. Two of his crew performed the unusual distinctions of ditching successfully and baling out of their Mosquito safely. Wing Commander Lambert – soon to be decorated with the Distinguished Flying Cross and Distinguished Service Order in comparatively rapid order in recognition of his bravery and leadership – shared a hut with Sammy Hoare and Sticky Murphy. He remembered the latter's raucous singing as he performed his ablutions in an adjoining room.

Late in 1943 and during the spring of 1944, the morale of Bomber Command was in a low state. Heavy losses were sustained nightly, the Germans now fighting like tigers as the pounding of their Fatherland brought early defeat nearer. Assorted night-fighter tactics and brave crews could hardly fail to deplete the hordes of Lancaster and Halifax bombers that poured across the much-battered Reich.

One of the enemy's main weapons that caused major losses was the Messerschmitt 110 with a pair of 'Schräge Musik' 20mm cannons firing upwards. The technique of German crews was to fly below the Allied bomber stream, pick out a target on a parallel course, and slide beneath to the blank spot of the aircraft, take careful aim and shoot off a wing. The corkscrewing of bombers, wearing but wise as an evasive procedure to avoid the slaughter, was countered by the night fighters, who carried out a similar manoeuvre in formation. Bomber Command's spirits fell as aircraft exploded without apparent cause.

During a period of about five months to March 1944, Bomber Command had been effectively 'wiped out' – but replaced. Some 1,047 aircraft had been lost and 1,682 damaged. Disaster threatened the offensive, which was a fundamental bastion of the Allied effort. Drastic protective and counter measures were essential if the offensive was to continue. The Nuremberg raid, with more than 100 bombers lost out of about 800, was a defeat for Bomber Command on any terms. The bomber-power way to kill the German people's will to resist was in jeopardy.

Air Chief Marshal Sir Arthur Harris, Air Officer Commanding-in-Chief of Bomber Command, was calling out for night-flying Mosquito fighters 'on a substantial scale'. No. 100 Group of that Service was formed to attack enemy night fighters over Germany and protect Bomber Command's forces.

Great scientific advances had been made in forms of radar available, including one to enable Mosquitoes to home in on German night-fighter radar. This was a telling reverse of the German technique of using radar in fighters to latch on to the Allied bombers when they had navigational and bombing-aid radar in operation. Many hours were flown by No. 100 Group night after night in adverse weather conditions – sometimes when bombers were not in the air. Complex plans were conceived and executed to inflict maximum damage. Squadrons operated at varying levels, radar-equipped fighters mixing with the bomber stream, and Nos 23 and 515 Squadrons concentrated on low-level intruding, lurking around enemy aerodromes, strafing and bombing. Experienced night-fighter crews were of the greatest value to Germany in her agony. Each one lost by RAF action counted out of all proportion because of personnel shortage. Whether shot down or given a touch of 'Moskitopanik', causing them to crash, was of little consequence to Bomber Command crews, whose protection grew apace.

No. 100 Group was commanded by Air Vice Marshal Addison, with Air Commodore Rory Chisholm his senior air staff officer. Addison was a scientist of long standing, radar and kindred aids having been studied for many years for defence and offence. Early in the war, as a wing commander, he had developed scientific assistance for aircrews and controllers, and by 1944 he had the experience, knowledge and mental agility to use his squadrons to greatest advantage.

Rory Chisholm was an ace night-fighter pilot of wide experience and reputation, who had also commanded an elite experimental outfit – the Fighter Development Unit.

A proliferation of operational types were carried out, including Flower, Mahmood, Serrate and Ranger, revealing the versatility and high state of training of the Mosquito crews. Many had been concerned with night fighters with radar who had not been permitted to invade enemy airspace before. Others were veteran intruders and the trainees of veterans at High Ercall OTU. All combined efforts to defend the heavy bomber squadrons.

'Standard' bombing raids were undertaken, with master bomber pilots being supplied by squadrons of No. 100 Group, as well as napalm fire bombs dropped on airfields and additional targets by Nos 23 and 515 and other squadrons. One particular Operation Firebash hit Hohn and Flensburg. American AI radar Mk XV, which became known as ASH, was fitted in place of machine guns in the Mk VI Mosquitoes of Nos 23 and 515 Squadrons, with fresh training to enable the navigators to operate this specialist equipment skilfully.

On the social side, No. 23 Squadron soon integrated with the local population and the men captured many hearts with their carefree temperament and attitude. However, after one slight misunderstanding at a neighbouring pub, when the 'Mediterranean spirit' of Sticky and others entering by the windows was not appreciated, they changed their allegiance and were gladly accepted at another hostelry.

The lads were good customers and the days of vermouth and wine by the half-pint receded in favour of a few pints of beer and the odd whisky. Sticky took his wife, when she lived in the vicinity, clutching her half-pint glass. He was determined that the squadron spirit should be maintained. It was a happy unit, reflecting the commanding officer's personality, and he intended to keep it so. Sticky made a point of welcoming fresh crews into the family circle, and insisted on spending his few leisure hours at sport or with his crewmen, or the local people. Jean gradually accepted this. It was part of her husband's devotion to the Service.

Sticky also attended the parish church, read the lesson, and often after church parade went to a Sunday cocktail party that a local resident gave for all-comers. His easy manner with all types, diplomatic attitude to Sammy Hoare's rather possessive stance towards No. 23 Squadron, and the station commander's stricter interpretation of the word 'discipline', all contributed to happy days. One of Sticky's favourite tricks was to throw thunderflashes down chimney tops to explode in the cast-iron stoves. He was the first to laugh when the same thing was done to him, even when, on one occasion, he was taking a disciplinary hearing against an airman. He returned to dismiss the charge, seeing how incongruous any other result would be.

Sticky was delayed in arriving at one Sunday cocktail party, having been flying late the night before. Captain Joe Cooper, DFC, recalled in Jersey in 1975: 'Someone asked Sticky if he had had any joy the previous night. "Yes," he replied, "I got back."' His unusually laconic tone may have indicated that he thought it was not the time or place for 'shop talk', or was a sign to other veterans that he knew that luck did not continue forever.

One of Sticky's great pleasures was the friendship he found with Mr
and Mrs Whitehead of Little Snoring Farm, which enclosed part of the
aerodrome. The husband was a sympathetic soul when it came to a party,
while wife Bessie cooked Norfolk specialities for Sticky – who had provided much of the flour, sugar, raisins, lard etc. from mess sources – and
other lads. They relaxed together and the Whiteheads appreciated Sticky's
qualities as a person.

The former Flight Lieutenant Buddy Badley, DFC, a Kiwi and kindred
spirit of Murphy, recalled:

You could pick out Sticky Murphy immediately in a crowded bar. He
was either twisting the tips of his moustache, or an elbow was raised
higher than his glass as he took a sip. A bullet through his neck had
caused him to do this, and perhaps I had better qualify the remark
about the elbow being higher than anyone else's, because he was
usually surrounded by members of his squadron who all mimicked
his elevated elbow, so that it became a habit to hold their drinks in
that manner.

I can only remember one occasion when Sticky had to use his rank
to get the members of his squadron to obey. In terms of guns per
square metre, German airfields were perhaps the most heavily
defended areas. They could throw up an awesome concentration of
flak in a comparatively small area. As a result, losses and damage to
aircraft attacking them were heavy, and it became a court-martial
offence to attack an aerodrome without specific orders to do so. No. 23
Squadron must have had a blanket clearance since it was the main job
of the squadron by night.

One day we were asked to carry out a squadron effort against one
such airfield during daytime. The first hedgehopping Mosquito to go
in would probably have had the element of surprise in its favour, but
the last one was going to have a very warm reception. Sticky insisted
upon being the last on this raid, whereas the rest of the squadron
insisted just as firmly that the place for the commanding officer was
by tradition at the head of the force. Sticky had to issue a direct order
to get his way.

Squadron Leader Rabone and Flying Officer Johns, his navigator, transferred to No. 23 Squadron from No. 515, and had arranged to go on a Day Ranger with Buddy Badley. Each pilot was to check early morning weather conditions and call the other – taking it in turns – if cloud cover seemed available. On 23 July 1944, Paul Rabone failed to call Buddy, but took off to attack targets in Denmark. He and Johns failed to return. Air-sea rescue flights were unable to find any trace of their aircraft over the North Sea.

Affiliation flights simulating fighter strikes took place with Liberators of No. 223 Squadron. The four-engined aircraft pilots took fright when seeing how vulnerable they were to cannon attack, viewed from the Mosquito navigator's seat.

Flying Officer George Stewart and Paul Beaudet of the Royal Canadian Air Force were characters. George was a devoted pilot, and remained so into 1978. He flew several Mosquitoes to No. 23 Squadron in Sardinia, determined to get on to operations on the squadron, but was sent back each time. Unabashed he persisted, and then made his mark and was called 'Regardless' for determinedly pressing on against all odds and circumstances, presumed to have a 'death wish'. He practised dogfights with any passing aircraft, preferably American, when doing night-flying tests, and attacked as long as his ammunition lasted out when over enemy territory. In about six months this crew carried out fifty operational sorties and were award the DFC.

On two successive days in August 1944, Wing Commander Sticky Murphy led formations of Nos 23 and 515 Squadrons (fourteen from No. 23 alone) to support Lancasters attacking Bordeaux Docks, at Mosquito maximum range, requiring landing in south-west England. George Stewart was delayed by engine trouble, but blithely followed his nickname by flying alone across the Cherbourg Peninsula and Brittany, at low level, to join the others. He was quite excited at being shot at angrily by American tank columns who naturally resented anything that flew near them. Only the Royal Navy had been found to be more resentful, and even more accurate with longer practice.

Jock Reid wrote:

I well recall when 23 and 515 Squadrons were detailed to act as high-level escort to a force of Lancaster bombers attacking the oil storage depot at Pauillac, near Bordeaux. It was a 'bolt from the blue'. I was living off the camp with my wife at a house in Fakenham on the Holt Road, and our bedroom was upstairs facing the main road. On the morning of 4 August at 3.30am, I awoke to hear small gravel hitting our window. Flight Lieutenant Bill Gregory was standing beside a van on the road outside, and I dressed hurriedly and he drove me into the camp. I there learned that we were to go on a daylight raid with 450 Lancasters to Bordeaux and we were to fly low to avoid radar and then climb to 15,000ft on target.

There was a real panic on as we had no maps of the area, and we were to leave at 07.00 hours. The weather had been bad at night with low cloud (haar) affecting the usual operations, so we had been switched to daytime operations. It was postponed in the morning, but we eventually took off later in the afternoon. Rendezvous time was 16.00 hours and the target indicators were to go down at 18.08 hours.

We had twenty-four aircraft in formations of three, flying at o feet to Land's End, few of the pilots having had much practice in formation, and we had no maps. We had no radar aids at our height and had to keep radio telephone silence. All the navigators were leaving it to the leading aircraft, which was ours, with Sticky commanding the formation. We kept well out at sea around Ushant, but saw one aircraft which turned tail and disappeared in a cloud of smoke. As rendezvous time approached, there was still no sign of the bombers and we were too low to see any distance. With great relief we saw the swarm beginning to climb ahead of us, and climbing away above them we had a great view of the attack and listened to the remarks of the Pathfinders marking with flares, even in daylight. The call to attack came from the Master Bomber and they had a scramble to get their bombs away and I am sure the target area was cleared at 6.30pm, and we set course for England, landing at Winkleigh in Devon, as we had insufficient fuel to get back to base and in any case the 'haar' sea mist had come in over Norfolk once more.

The party in the mess was a memorable one and I recall a number of debagged personnel in the bar before retiring to bed.

The next day we returned to Pauillac at the same time with 400

Lancasters. This time we shortened the trip by cutting across the Brest Peninsula so that the route was Start Point–Lannion–Lorient at ground level, and this leg proved much more eventful. We had trouble with the Allied navies off the coast and the United States forces had broken out of the beachhead at Avranches and were sweeping along the main road to Brest. They took umbrage at our approach and luckily we spotted the big crane at Lorient in time to go round to the west to avoid a naval base there, but noticed a few surprised sentries on some of the gun positions as we flew over at low level. There was some heavy flak from the Isle of Groix which was accurate enough to hit one of our formation, but he flew alongside as Sticky asked him to do and was examined for damage, but there was no sign of any serious damage.

The bombing attack went off well and again we were at high level and some enemy aircraft were sighted but they avoided any contact and headed away from the main force. I believe that the monitors in the UK were reporting that they said they had made no contact with the bomber force.

The main attack was preceded by one aircraft which descended to low level and dropped a stick of bombs on a tanker moored in the estuary. The explosion of the bombs paralleled the length of the ship, narrowly missing it, and before leaving the area, we saw that the ship was heeled over on its side.

We returned to England and landed at Colerne, near Bath, returning to Little Snoring the next morning where the low cloud had not lifted and Sticky proceeded to lead the formation down through 500ft of cloud, the first time we had had the doubtful pleasure of performing that manoeuvre.

One rather frightening episode was the night of 5 September 1944 when we did an intruder to Parchim and got involved with the airfield defences at Hagenow, having played cat and mouse with the decoy airfield in the vicinity. Having established which was the decoy and which was the real aerodrome, we avoided crossing the latter, but after investigating a flashing light which appeared to be that of aircraft identification lights, we crossed the main airfield at about 1,000ft and were coned by searchlights and came under intense light flak. Sticky's reaction on these occasions was to put everything down into the right-hand corner, and sort of peel off. It was rather low for this and I recall trees and tracer flashing past as I shouted a warning about height. I think this was the nearest we ever came to death together. He always wore one of Jean's silk stockings round his neck, and I carried a small wooden doll, an airman, inside my tunic for luck. It was sodden after that lot, and I was sure we had had it.

Squadron Leader Charles Price, station intelligence officer, was very busy with the various tactics and ploys as well as being concerned with the monitoring of enemy transmissions and all types of intelligence material. He recalled in February 1975:

Although I had not known Sticky Murphy for a very long time, we were very close. Close 'in business' and 'off duty'. It is only the mess and 'off-duty' life I can recount! Sticky prided himself on being a sophisticated raconteur and a fellow who would have a bet on anything. He and I had a nightly 'half dollar' bet as to whether the squadron would operate or not the next day/night. We had a string pulley device suspended from the ceiling of the mess bar; on one end of the string was a large dice and on the other end of the string a scrubbing brush. If the squadron had been deputed to operate, the dice end was pulled down. It's horrible I know but we were younger than now. We called this 'dicing with Jesus'. If the operation was 'scrubbed' due to, say, weather, tactics etc., the brush was pulled down ('scrubbed'). I think Sticky and I finished about equal on our betting transactions.

Sticky amassed and saved very pertinent yarns (specially for me). Knowing I was in local government in civil life – I was a Town Clerk – the jokes he liked telling for my benefit and to take the Michael, were of the local government variety, such as: 'The Parks Superintendent, after holidaying in Venice, suggested to his committee that they should buy a gondola and put it on the lake. One old councillor, a little out of his depth, said, "I agree with the Parks Superintendent, but while we are about it, let's buy two and breed from them."'

Sticky enjoyed recalling a north of England cemetery committee discussing whether or not to spend £16 in connection with the consecration of a further portion of the cemetery. This was opposed by one Councillor who stated that he could not understand why the cemetery should be consecrated and, anyway, if the Council decided to do the work, he knew it would cost a lot more than £16 because he had just had his back yard done.

Sticky also loved quoting a finance committee (again in the north of England) discussing the granting of an honorarium to a workman who had been in the Council's employ for a great number of years. One Councillor interrupted the debate by saying, 'What's the use of giving 'im and 'onorarium, 'e couldn't play it if 'e 'ad it.'

At 1am on the night of 30/31 August 1944, Sticky Murphy arrived at the Castle Hotel, Norwich, by car, and stepped smartly into the restaurant, feeling full of the joys. 'What's on?' he asked. 'I'm on,' said the waitress, whereupon the CO remarked, 'Goodness gracious me, step into the kitchen.' The squadron diarist recorded this story with some trepidation.

During July Sticky and Jock carried out four sorties, intruding on aerodromes in Belgium, France and Germany, and similarly on targets in August – the exceptional one being to Peenemünde (home of V-weapon development) on 29 August, which took five hours and thirty minutes, much of it in cloud. This flight to the Baltic Sea beyond Denmark was at the greatest possible range of the Mosquito VI, and shortly afterwards the same area was visited in an intruder trip to Lübeck.

All crews were impressed during the summer of 1944 by the fires from Bomber Command's 'heavies' attacks on Germany, and by the intense flak, which they shared with the Lancasters ranging across the Fatherland. At 4am one morning six aircraft of the squadron took off in quick succession and bombed targets from 20,000 feet – rather stratospheric by intruder standards. It was a new idea to draw up the night fighters and then attack them utilising the more efficient radar system that had been installed.

By the autumn of 1944 few crews from the late Malta days, or from Sardinian times, survived. Kit Cotter, a sergeant in the New Zealand Air Force, had become a flying officer with a Distinguished Flying Cross and had carried out sixty-five sorties. In his cups one night he confided to a comrade that he only felt truly alive when flying on operations and wished

to continue, but was instead rested. It was realised that a strong desire
to press on and on and on was one sign of the need for a break from the
pressure. Lank hair and a pallor of skin regardless of sunshine, together
with listlessness and difficulty in staying awake, were recognisable signs
that mental and physical exhaustion were present. If ignored, failure to
return, or a flying accident, often occurred.

Buddy Badley, the other Kiwi, made a fourth return flight on one
engine, from Copenhagen this time, and his long tour of aggressive sorties
was also rewarded with a DFC.

By the end of November, Sticky had flown a total of eighty-eight operations, including fifty-two while on No. 23 Squadron, and his 'rest' and
Staff College threatened daily. During that month he had flown with
Flight Lieutenant Reid on a Day Ranger in company with Group Captain
Sammy Hoare on 1 November, beginning at 2pm. France was scoured
and an hour spent in the vicinity of Juvincourt Aerodrome, but poor
weather and visibility brought no reward.

Flight Lieutenant Reid explained: 'I was getting a bit browned off at
Little Snoring. Sticky had been CO of the squadron for almost a year,
and I thought he was prolonging his stay by flying only occasionally.
"Binding again" − I pointed out to him that the gaps between our trips
meant, to my mind, that every one was like a first one − you got out of
practice. I wanted to get on with my tour and finish with it, as it had
already been extended beyond the usual quota.'

At a party on 24 November, Bill Gregory, squadron navigation officer,
was gingerly dancing with a lady whose ankle was in plaster. Sticky could
not stand this, and he excused Bill, saying, 'Pull your finger out, Bill' and
swept the injured lady off her feet, plaster as well, in an energetic polka.

Gütersloh Aerodrome, about 130 miles into Germany from the Zuider
Zee, was headquarters of the German night-fighter force. Flying Officer
Eastwood made a sortie there and did not return.

On the morning of 2 December 1944, Flight Lieutenant Jock Reid had
considerable inflammation of his ears and was grounded by the squadron
medical officer until further orders. Just after leaving sick quarters he met
his pilot, Sticky, and they were not expecting to operate that night, but
Sticky had decided to do so. Jock told him of the doc's verdict and Wing
Commander Murphy happily replied: 'Not to worry, I'll find another

navigator.' This was unusual on operations, and not to Jock's liking. It was recognised that crews combined well after months together.

Shortly before, Richard Dimbleby had recorded Sticky's comments on return from a sortie for BBC radio news. Sticky said: 'No joy, I'm afraid. The weather was filthy as usual, but we reached our target and promptly threw our bombs on it. I think we hit the intersections of the runways, but could not be sure because of the flak and searchlights!'

Eight crews went off on the night of 2 December, Sticky telephoning Jean to say: 'Just one more trip, darling. A wing commander's moon tonight.' He was not concerned about favourable operating conditions and chose as his target the notorious Gütersloh, taking a young, keen flight sergeant, Douglas Darbon, with him as navigator. Darbon was a man of strict principles, and a Boy Scout in his younger days. He was now twenty-one and came from Charlton in south-east London. Nine crews of No. 23 Squadron flew that night, in bright moonlight, the other eight claiming seven locomotives damaged and rolling stock attacked.

Wing Commander Murphy and Flight Sergeant Darbon took off during the evening, and flew via the Zuider Zee. What success they had is unknown, but at 11.15pm when returning home in Mosquito 'Z for Zebra', and in sight of the Zuider Zee, they plunged into the ground near Oldebroek in the Netherlands, on heathland similar to parts of the New Forest. The aircraft was shattered, both men were killed, and were buried by local workmen.

At the very time of the crash, Wing Commander Murphy's mother was stricken by excruciating pains at home at 'Morland'. These gradually passed as her daughter Doreen rushed to her aid. Mrs Ethel Murphy remained convinced that her son lived for the duration of her agony. As the Air Ministry telegram and other details came to the family, times and dates were checked. Sammy Hoare and George Heycock cared for Jean Murphy and Gail, who were at Little Snoring.

To his squadron, their commanding officer had seemed indestructible. Everyone was shocked, even used to casualties as they were. Mosquitoes flew on air-sea rescue patrols, and these continued until the weather worsened considerably. Hope passed of rescue at sea, and the Squadron Diary records: 'It is with very deep regret we report that Wing Commander Murphy and Flight Sergeant Darbon failed to return.

He had been our CO for almost a year, and prior to that was a flight commander. His enthusiasm and irrepressible spirit were a joy, and inspiration to everybody – a grand CO and a very fine friend to all – we sincerely hope that news may come that both he and Flight Sergeant Darbon are safe.'

That night, 110 aircraft of No. 100 Group were active over Europe on a variety of raids. A few weeks before, Wing Commander Guy Gibson, VC, DSO. DFC, had crashed with Squadron Leader Lawrence in a Mosquito at Steenbergen, not far from Sticky Murphy's last resting place. Buddy Badley remembered:

In our mess, each man put £5.00 into a kitty at the bar, so that if he did not return the boys could have a drink on him. With a few exceptions, the intelligence officer was known for his accurate predictions as to who and when people were going to 'buy it'.

If you were on this list, and had to force-land elsewhere and became overdue, it was important to get to a telephone quickly to save your £5.00, as everybody knew where you had gone, and what your endurance was as far as fuel was concerned.

Although by the law of averages Sticky should have been at the head of the list, to the best of my knowledge he was not on it at all. Perhaps evidence of the lucky streak had dictated this.

When it was learned that Sticky was overdue, nobody wanted to believe that the worst could have happened, and there was no suggestion of broaching his kitty. This would have meant that we had given up hope. Only after the whole of the United Kingdom had been checked for a missing Mosquito, and only after it became obvious that Sticky was not coming back, did the squadron go on the biggest wake in its history.

Singing the songs, including 'Here's to the Next Man to Die!' in the contemporary manner of bravado, the mess echoed as all grieved in their way. Even more, it was a shock and blow to the people of Little Snoring, who had grown to know Sticky as a jovial character who epitomised the best qualities of the Royal Air Force.

On the afternoon of 2 December, wearing United States parachutist's boots that he had acquired, Sticky had gone shooting and had a chat with the local gamekeeper about prospects and the weather.

Legends grew at Little Snoring, among Service and civilian personnel alike. Suspicions were voiced that Sticky had not really disappeared without official knowledge. His clandestine earlier career was suspected, and SOE or the Secret Service had arranged it all, rumour said. Wing Commander Murphy had been seen in London, gossip had it, by the friend of a friend who was also unidentifiable, who had failed to speak to him in the street there. There was of course no truth to these rumours, but they grew until his grave was found in late 1945.

Within hours of his loss, notification arrived of the award of the Bar to his Distinguished Service Order, in these terms: 'Since being awarded the Distinguished Service Order this officer has participated in a large number of sorties involving attacks on a wide range of targets. In these operations, Wing Commander Murphy has most effectively attacked many enemy locomotives; he has also been responsible for the destruction of two enemy aircraft and very many mechanical vehicles during the period. His outstanding skill, gallant leadership, and iron determination, have been reflected in the fine fighting qualities of his squadron, which has won much success.'

The war had to go on, and the now Wing Commander Phil Russell, DFC, became commanding officer, saying later: 'I felt very much the understudy taking the place of the star.'

In seventeen months of operations, Mosquitoes of No. 100 Group flew 7,884 sorties. Enemy aircraft claimed as destroyed in flight amounted to 249, and 18 on the ground, for the loss of 69 Mosquitoes. Bomber Command pressed on until war ended, despite casualties in the tens of thousands, many having no known graves.

Chapter Ten

Tributes to Sticky

Tributes to Wing Commander Sticky Murphy are set out in alphabetical order, illustrating the variety of those he knew during his life, and the agreement in admiration of his personality and qualities. Brief particulars are given of each contributor.

David Atherton was a navigator on No. 23 Squadron in Sardinia and at Little Snoring, who carried out many operational sorties with his pilot, Flight Sergeant Bert Southey. David later became a squadron leader in the Royal Air Force, and in Civvy Street became a senior civil servant. In 1977 he wrote:

I remember Sticky – his infectious smile, his long elegance, his bright twinkling adventurous eyes, and his Croix de Guerre ribbon, with the others, when, much a junior, I happened to be beside him and Micky Martin at the bar at Little Snoring. They must have been at least 27 at the time!

I remember him in his dressing gown on the front outside the half-built ex-Italian Air Force block at Fertilia in Sardinia, where we lived, lending 'zip and sparkle' to the morning scene. The types around – 'The Baron', baggy shorts, great flabby white chest, huge beaming red face, off to borrow Sticky's Jeep for some expedition. Then Griffiths, a suave character later to be our flight commander, with Buddy Badley, Kit Cotter and the rest cocking rifles to shoot at seagulls.

I was not one of the responsible ones who managed the inner

Doreen and Alan Murphy.
(Doreen Gravestock)

Alan and George Murphy, circa 1933.
(Jean Bunting)

'B' Squadron, first term, RAF Cranwell, September 1936. *(Jean Bunting)*

Flight Cadet Murphy, RAF College Cranwell. *(Jean Bunting)*

Sticky's caption to this picture read, 'Oo done it. My story is that a gust caught me and I'm sticking to it.' *(Jean Bunting)*

Rugger at Cranwell, Sticky with the ball. *(Jean Bunting)*

(Below and right) Flying Officer Alan 'Sticky' Murphy. *(Doreen Gravestock)*

Wedding day of Jean and Sticky Murphy, Newbury, September 1941. *(Jean Bunting)*

Squadron Leader Nesbitt-Dufort's pranged black Lysander at Issoudun, France. Photographed by the Resistance in late January 1942 after a seven hour flight to rescue 'BRICK' and 'ST JACQUES'. *(Peter Coley)*

Westland Lysander. *(Peter Coley)*

Squadron Leader Murphy DSO, DFC, outside Buckingham Palace with Flight Officer Murphy WAAF and Junior Commander Doreen Murphy ATS (his sister). *(Doreen Gravestock)*

Squadron Leader John Nesbitt-Dufort with 'BRICK' and 'St JACQUES' French officers rescued with him by Sticky Murphy in an Anson sortie of March 1942. *(Nesbitt-Dufort collection)*

No. 23 Squadron Mosquito flying close to Malta. *(Peter Coley)*

Pilot Officer Harry 'Tich' Cossar DFC who accompanied Sticky Murphy in the Anson rescue trip in March 1942 deep inside France. First twin-engine landing at night by Special Duty Squadron. *(H. Cossar)*

Colonel (then Major) Jean Cassart, after return from Germany. *(Mme Navarre)*

(Below) Brigadier Juliusz Kleeberg who was rescued by Sticky Murphy in the Anson, March 1942, when he was commanding Polish Secret Forces in France. *(Polish Institue)*

(Above) Jean Cassart and Jim Coley at Neufchâteau in 1975, where Sticky Murphy was ambushed. *(Peter Coley)*

(Left) Flight Lieutenant Bill Shattock, Jim Coley's pilot. *(W.S. Shattock)*

No, 23 Squadron Mosquito, Malta. *(T. Cushing)*

Bill Shattock (left) and Jim Coley (right) 'with three of our erks', 15 September 1943. *(Peter Coley)*

FEBRUARY, 1944.

Date	Hour	Aircraft Type and No.	Pilot	Duty
1/2/44	1500	Mosquito HX900	F/Sgt. SHATTOCK.	NAVIGATOR & W/OP.
1/2/44	2100	LR253	— " —	— " —
3/2/44	1410	LR252	— " —	— " —
3/2/44	2125	LR252	— " —	— " —
5/2/44	1510	LR252	— " —	— " —
7/2/44	1545	HJ765	— " —	— " —
9/2/44	1445	HJ765	— " —	— " —
9/2/44	1955	HJ765	— " —	— " —
			SP Russell — S/LDR.	
			O/C. "B" FLIGHT.	
			Sam K. Murphy — W/CDR.	
			O/C. 23 SQUADRON.	

Jim Coley's logbook entries, from February 1944, signed off by Sticky Murphy. *(Peter Coley)*

ALGHERO, SARDINIA.

REMARKS (including results of bombing, gunnery, exercises, etc.)	Flying Times	
	Day	Night
N.F.T.	·25	
(1) INTRUDER – MARSEILLE AREA – 10/10		2·25
A.C. S/L's. OVER MARS. (?) ROCKET(S) IN AIR 'SHORTYS' N/F.		
N.F.T.	·50	
(2) INTRUDER – PERPIGNAN, MONTPELLIER,		4·05
ISTRES (MARS.) — (NEUTRAL (?) SPAIN WELL		
LIT UP) – HOSPITAL SHIP GULF OF BEAUNE,		
NO JOY INCL. AVIGNON + NIMES. TERRIFIC		
RATE BLOWING.		
N.F.T.	·15	
N.F.T.	·20	
N.F.T.	·15	
(3) OFFENSIVE PATROL – ROME / LA SPECIA		2·50
GRIM WEATHER EN ROUTE; LAST ONE'S		
HERE. VITERB./GROSS. INACTIVE. HUN ASLEEP.		
TOTAL MONTHLY FLYING TIMES	1·45	9·20
OPERATIONAL SORTIES — 3.		
TOTAL SORTIES — 26.		
TOTAL OPS. HOURS – 110·20. TOTAL TIME ...	187·50	185·35

(Below) Jim Coley and Sticky Murphy.
(Peter Coley)

**(Right) Squadron Leader Sticky Murphy
DSO, DFC, C de G. Summer of 1943
before leaving for Malta.** *(Jean Bunting)*

WE'VE DONE IT AGAIN

Photograph pasted in to Jim Coley's logbook, March 1944, Alghero, Sardinia. *(Peter Coley)*

From left to right, Jim Coley, D. Twitt, A. Yates, E. Layh, P. Burton-Gyles, Sticky Murphy, C. Hefford. Walking past the burnt-out structure of a German troop carrier. Italy, circa 1943. *(Peter Coley collection)*

No. 23 Squadron at Pomigliano d'Arco, near Naples, December 1943. Left to right, Jock Reid, F/O Robertson, Jim Coley, Sticky Murphy, F/Lt Bilbe-Robinson, Norman Conquer. *(Peter Coley collection)*

No. 23 Squadron, RAF Little Snoring. Officers past and present with traditional digits elevated salute, including S/Ldr Paul Rabone, S/Ldr Jock Brown, Group G/C Sammy Hoare (unelevated digit), G/C George Haycock, W/Cdr Sticky Murphy (highest digit). *(T. Cushing)*

Wing Commander Alan Murphy DSO, DFC, C de G, and Group Captain R. O'Bryen (Sammy) Hoare, DSO, DFC, and Harold Whitehead a local farmer on the right. *(T. Cushing)*

'Diceing tonight' (as opposed to scrubbed) demonstrated in the Little Snoring Mess by W/Cdr Sticky Murphy with F/Lt Griffiths 'facing the camera as usual'. *(Hawker Siddely)*

No. 23 Squadron, 29 October 1944. Sticky Murphy on the extreme left. *(Peter Coley)*

Oldebroek General Cemetery, Holland, circa 1952. *(Jean Bunting)*

Left to right, Jim Coley, Tom Cushing, Norman Conquer. Mayflower House, Little Snoring, August 1974. *(T. Cushing)*

working of the squadron. I just flew, listened, chatted, drank, picking up all the tips I could. But Sticky was a presence all of us felt directly, persuasively, charmingly and – bravely. He never seemed to lecture or coldly reprove. He was an example.

The nearest parallel it now seems to me, and it may not be so strained a parallel, would be Odysseus – the youngest, wisest, greatest leader of all the Greeks at Troy. He took his men to the ends of the earth, to the land of the Cyclops and to Circe's Isle.

Most of us, I think, would have gone there for Sticky. In the middle of the night as usual, with cloud all murky and grey in dim starlight. If he had chalked it up on the board in the briefing room one evening and told us why. Naturally we would have marked the flak areas in red on the charts, worked out the courses and distances, and got the wind forecasts.

Sticky would have strapped the Mosquito around his bottom, and soared off with the rest of us in a line, moving along the taxi track behind him.

We did not have a dull, leaden-spirited squadron as I suppose it could have been. You could not, with Sticky. He must have been one of the greatest operational leaders of the war.

Squadron Leader John Austin, DFC and Bar, Netherlands Flying Cross and Croix de Guerre, recalled in 1976:

I was posted to 1419 Flight from 51 Squadron in March 1941 as a sergeant pilot. Sticky Murphy was a flight lieutenant then and the first person in the flight to fly with me. I was of course flying Whitleys not Lysanders, and so the half-dozen times we flew together were when I ferried him around the UK, usually to Tangmere, and I see that he signed my logbook in November 1941 shortly before I went off to the Middle East.

When we were stationed at Newmarket I remember helping to lay out a triangle of lights and holding a torch as the apex to signal while Sticky practised night landings. His flying was always very precise, although he adopted a casual air when on the ground.

Sticky was always a great chap to be with and it made no difference

to him that I was a sergeant at that time. Later when my commission
came through he treated me exactly the same.

These are a few details which I recall after thirty-five years.

Captain Buddy Badley, DFC, of British Airways, a 'Jumbo Jet' pilot,
recollected in 1976:

Few who knew Sticky could help but like the man. His rather
mischievous grin was, at its widest, almost as broad as his moustache,
which lifted noticeably with his smile to heighten a happy countenance.
His eyes matched his grin.

He enjoyed the war with all the excitement it offered and with signs
of the European battle coming to an end he had every intention of
going out and lending a hand in the Far East, although he had already
done far more trips than the powers that be asked of a pilot.

No. 23 Squadron was not like other fighter squadrons. Its job was
intruding where each plane went out entirely on its own. Sometimes
one was asked to do a specific job but the planning and execution was
left entirely to the crew concerned. Most of the work was to a loose
overall plan, but in between we went out and did our own thing
anyway. By the very nature of its work, No. 23 Squadron was more a
collection of individualists than a regimented force.

To command successfully such an outfit called for some very special
qualities. Sticky was most successful. He was the supreme individualist.
He had scant regard for 'bull' and did not need rank to command.
Everyone who served under him liked and admired him so much and
had this sort of respect for the man rather than the rank. He had only
to suggest or ask and rarely to issue an order. He never asked anyone
to do anything that he was not prepared to do himself.

Charles Bovill, CEng, MIEE, FIERE, MRAeS, a 'boffin' on No. 1419
Flight with Sticky during 1941, commented in 1976:

I am delighted to say my little piece about Sticky Murphy. What a nice
chap he was, and how sad he should have perished. I remember him
so well. He used to laugh at my white flying overall, although it did

enable me to report the uncalled for rapid descent of a Whitley at
Graveley one night, impeccably dressed, when all the rest of the crew
were covered in the filth which seems to accompany a pile-up.

On the night of 28 October 1941 I went with Sticky Murphy and John
Nesbitt-Dufort on one of those SOE things – Operation Claude –
with Sticky piloting and John sitting in the seat beside him. I was on
the 'S for Sugar' phone which I developed and was operating. This
was from Newmarket and the aircraft was a Whitley V.

I was in civilian guise as an SOE man and not commissioned in the
RAF until some months later. Neither of these chaps knew anything
about me, and were so very kind and solicitous for my well-being,
giving me a sort of pacifying commentary about what they were doing.
I think they imagined that I had never been in an aircraft before. I well
remember their soothing comments when we were held in searchlights, which is, I suppose, a bit alarming. It is very difficult to describe
how people can be kind and considerate, but what they did not know
was that I had been one of the heads of the air department of Marconi's
for some years before, and I never told this to Sticky or John.

In those days we really liked our parents and had a feeling of
responsibility towards them. We were all richer for knowing Sticky
and John and their like.

Air Vice Marshal Sir Alan Boxer, KCVO, CB, DSO, DFC, an SOE pilot
with Sticky Murphy and commander of No. 161 Squadron (Special
Operations), remembered:

I served only briefly with Sticky Murphy and was transferred after
three months in No. 161 Squadron to command a flight in No. 138.
For reasons which now escape me, I recall that on one occasion I was
detailed to fly with Sticky on a Whitley sortie to central France –
I don't believe that either he or I had a very clear idea why we had
been crewed together, but I do know that he had never had the benefit
of any instruction on this rather cumbersome flying machine. No
doubt 'Mouse' Fielden had his reasons (CO of the squadron then)
but three things stand out in my memory.

Firstly the mission was completed successfully without the

interruption of enemy action; secondly, it seems (even then) extraordinary that an operational sortie was considered an appropriate time to be gaining initial experience on type; and thirdly, on landing we stalled at quite a height, and our arrival was jarring. It is my recollection of the Whitley that its one great attribute was its immensely strong undercarriage.

When I returned to command No. 161 he had left, so that this single episode was my only real contact with a charming man whose panache and reputation were recognised by us all.

Mrs Jean Bunting, formerly Murphy, née Leggat, Sticky's widow, called to mind:

My most vivid recollection of my husband, after thirty years, was his inherent sense of humour, irresistible charm and disarming sense of the ridiculous, which frequently landed him in trouble, and invariably renewed the morale of his fellows. As this book recounts on several occasions, even when there was nothing between him and death but the flimsy shell of an aeroplane and a little hostile fresh air, he could still evoke a laugh, however desperate, from those in contact with him. Physically tall, and built like the athlete he was, Sticky possessed the type of light blue eyes often associated with the sea: they had a twinkle in them that displayed the effervescent personality beneath. He had the capability of enjoying every second of his life with such zest it was contagious. These qualities were handed down to his daughter, born six months before he was posted as missing, and were to prove then, and later, to be of inestimable value to me.

His reckless courage was well known, and he achieved near impossible feats with an apparent ease that belied the training, skill and determination that lay behind them. His sense of patriotism and dedication to the Service was almost an obsession, and took precedence completely over his personal and private life. As his wife I could truthfully say he was married primarily to the Royal Air Force and secondly to me, and as I was also a member of that Service it seemed a natural state of affairs to me.

The memory of my love for the man, and the prolonged anguish of his, then, uncertain death, have inevitably softened with time. I would not resurrect them, even if it were in my power to do so, but there are many alive today who will remember, and in doing so feel the richer for having known him. I count myself privileged to have had more than most.

Air Commodore Roderick Chisholm, CBE, DSO, DFC, was a night-fighter 'ace' and one of the commanders of No. 100 (Bomber Support) Group of Bomber Command. He recollected: 'I knew Sticky Murphy, and can remember him as a brave, happy and engaging chap, with a great record.'

Wing Commander Norman Conquer, OBE, was one of Sticky's navigators in Malta, Sicily, Italy, Sardinia and at Little Snoring. He remembered:

Sticky Murphy's main characteristics, or rather those which remain indelibly printed on my memory of him, were zest, enthusiasm, ebullience and tenacity. They were manifest in his whole attitude to our life at those times.

Intruder operations were essentially 'lonely', and so I was never able to observe him in action against the enemy; but in organising our activities, moving the squadron about the Mediterranean, and back through North Africa to the UK (in whole or several parts), in setting up new quarters or obtaining supplies, in flying, servicing or admin matters and, above all, at play, I remember his unflagging energy, his exuberance – and his ever-present neighing laugh! He enjoyed himself hugely, whether organising maximum effort against northern Italy on a fine night, full 'attack' on the local town establishments at 2am on a dirty night, or all available guns against formations of wild duck on a calm evening – the Fertilia barrage!

Life was grim for many in 1943/44, and had its dull, fearful, tragic moments for the members of No. 23 Squadron also, but Sticky inspired in all those around him gaiety without frivolity, daring without abandon, and conformity without servility. In short, he was a natural leader of men.

Mrs Lily Graham, née Young, of Workington, Cumbria, had this to say about Sticky: 'I was the nanny when Alan Murphy was born in 1917, and remember him and his family really well, although I am now over eighty years of age [when this account was given]. They were lovely people, and Alan was a very energetic baby. I had to hold him still in the studio, while a photograph was taken with his sister Doreen. I followed his career with great interest until he made the supreme sacrifice.'

Mrs Doreen Gravestock, née Murphy, only sister of Sticky Murphy, then living with husband Peter and children Michael and Alison at Barton Seagrave, was pleased to recall:

At my wedding in 1942 to Peter Gravestock in London, Dennis King was also Peter's best man. After the reception six of us – Jean, Sticky, Dennis, Sheila (my sister-in-law), Peter and I – went in a taxi to Paddington. About halfway there the taxi broke down, just in front of a bus queue. My (very new) husband got out to repair the taxi. Dennis was waving his hands about trying to get another taxi, and Sticky just walked up and down the bus queue telling everyone that if his new brother-in-law didn't get the taxi going, we were going to miss the train to Cornwall.

There was a look of blank astonishment on the faces of the people in the queue, who thought he was raving mad. I might add that we just caught the train, with Dennis pushing the luggage in after us, just as the train was moving off.

I told everyone who knew where we were going for our honeymoon, not to give Sticky the address, but by some trickery he got it out of Sheila, and a very naughty telegram was waiting for us when we arrived.

The last time I saw Sticky was in November 1944. I left the ATS and my son was born the following March. Peter was still in the Army, so I went home to Ferndown, to find Sticky had come home for one night. I arrived home in a taxi, and Sticky came bounding down the drive saying, 'How is my pregnant sister?' The taxi driver's mouth fell open. The next day Sticky flew from Hurn, and was killed three weeks later.

I have been asked if he showed any incipient leadership, courage or daring when he was a boy. I can't honestly say that he showed great signs of leadership, but perhaps that was because I was the 'big sister', and in our happy childhood there was little opportunity to show courage.

He was certainly daring, as are most young boys, and did the usual cliff, rock and tree climbing. He liked to sail and swim when the sea was rough. He was quite fearless. Sticky found it very easy to communicate with people of all ages, and all walks of life, and I never knew him to be mean, petty or spiteful.

I am very proud to have been Sticky's sister. He had a wonderful zest for living, and when one was in his company, he made the ordinary things that happen in life seem more carefree, gay and interesting than anyone else I have known.

Air Commodore George Heycock, CB, AFC, was officer commanding No. 23 Squadron during the early war years, having John Nesbitt-Dufort and Sammy Hoare among his flight commanders. He recalled:

I was station commander at West Raynham, near Fakenham, and not far from Little Snoring, where Sticky Murphy commanded No. 23 Squadron which I had had the honour to command in the early years of the war.

Group Captain Sammy Hoare had been one of my flight commanders in those days at Ford, and when he and Sticky teamed up, I don't suppose one could have found a better team of dedicated pilots in their determination to get at the enemy.

With this 'passion' they both possessed a splendidly gay and cheerful personality. Tragically it was their consuming determination to complete their tasks, and never 'let up' which led to their deaths; in Sticky's case on his last mission, and at the very end of the flight by pressing home a daring attack at the lowest height in a defended area.

It is therefore hardly necessary to restate what everyone who knew Sticky realised, and that was the shining example of his sheer guts and bravery. I remember talking to him as his last few missions approached, and saying that I hoped he would 'lay off' being too venturesome. I recall him laughing this off, but saying he felt nervous of the fact, but he seemed elated too, and so had to press on.

I think I had some premonition, and indeed mentioned to the air officer commanding that it might be a good plan to cook up a reason to avoid him doing his 'last flight', but, of course, one could not do that, and so what many felt might happen, did take place.

There is no doubt that 'Sticky' was one of the band of super aircrews whose gallantry was outstanding, and whose living was an example to all us lesser people, yet of whom so many were gradually lost to the Service, and, indeed, to the nation.

Group Captain Ronald Hockey, DSO, DFC, was another pioneer SOE pilot, who recollected:

I was one of the first Whitley captains on No. 1419 Flight, and No. 138 Squadron. Sticky Murphy was my best friend during that time.

He was a first-class pilot, full of guts, and a great companion with a sense of humour and an irrepressible joy in living.

Sticky was a man who inspired all who came in contact with him to efforts which surprised even themselves. But behind that apparent 'devil-may-care' attitude was a cool, calculating mind, capable of assessing the problems and balancing them with the priorities.

Air Chief Marshal Sir Lewis Hodges, KCB, CBE, DSO, DFC, ADC, was a survivor of Sticky's Cranwell days, and a leading clandestine pick-up pilot and commander in later years. He remembered: 'Sticky Murphy was certainly a great character, and I knew him quite well. He was a cadet with me at Cranwell in 1937–38. As a cadet he was a great personality, and a great athlete, and he held the College long-jump record, which I believe stood for a good many years.'

Group Captain Brian Kingcome, DSO, DFC, was a fellow cadet at Cranwell with Sticky Murphy, and a Battle of Britain fighter 'ace'. He gladly contributed:

I last saw him in Italy in early 1944, when I was commanding a Spitfire wing near Naples, and he flew his Mosquito in for a drink. He had not changed. I don't think anything would have changed Sticky while life remained.

Wing Commander Frederick Lambert, DSO, DFC, former commander of No. 515 Squadron, wrote in April 1977:

For some months before he was killed in December 1944, I shared a billet with Sticky Murphy and Group Captain Sammy Hoare at RAF Station, Little Snoring.

I feel that Sticky typified the precision and efficiency of operational life of that era; and, in his case, backed by faultless flying perfection, at which profession he was a superb master.

I think he must have been an immensely fit man, for after a day's 'ops', Day Ranging over Germany (at which he excelled), he would proceed to play such sport as was going.

In his own way he was quite a family man and often told me of his cherished loved ones.

After this came his love of Cranwell and flying. Little Snoring and Norfolk will probably never see such exquisite single-engined flying again!

Mrs Rosemarie Lambert, née Swain, happily remembered in 1975 from her home in Fakenham:

I was one of five WAAFs attached to No. 23 Squadron at Little Snoring where I had been serving since November 1942. I drove transport for the squadron, which was the favourite of all of us. They were a lovely squadron. There was no doubt among us that they were above the others in style and reputation, and were a 'crack' squadron.

They were full of themselves when they arrived in 1944, and so happy under Wing Commander Sticky Murphy's leadership – they changed the atmosphere of the station. Previously No. 515 – the other Mosquito squadron had suffered heavy losses and morale was down. This revived with fresh crews including Wing Commander Lambert, and the famous Squadron Leader 'Micky' Martin.

Sticky was a 'smasher' – as we would say in those days – and such a happy contrast to some senior officers in his easy attitude towards all ranks. He made the ground crews feel part of the squadron family – as those who came back from the Middle East clearly did. This improved morale and produced a squadron spirit I had not previously known. The station commander, Group Captain 'Sammy' Hoare undoubtedly favoured No. 23 as his old squadron, and used to fly with them.

In early 1945 some airmen who were not tradesmen essential to aircraft maintenance were posted into the Army. They cried when they left No. 23 Squadron!

That winter there was a squadron party at Great Snoring, and a 70lb cheese was rolled down the road. Sticky was there as squadron CO. He was always so cheerful. His charm and concern for everybody's welfare made him outstanding in my memory.

I drove him out to his aircraft the night he went missing. It was a terrible shock to all of us when he did not come back. Nobody believed he was dead. There were all sorts of rumours that he had not been killed, but that it was part of his former special duty business. Various people claimed to have seen him in London, but were unable to speak to him.

There was a hell of a row one night because a flight lieutenant who was an administration officer, and who had a bigger moustache than Sticky, found himself, after a party, with one side of his moustache shaved off – leaving him lopsided with one 'wing' lower than the other. There were all sorts of threats to find the culprits, but it died down.

Nobody doubted that some of the No. 23 Squadron lads had done it.

Air Marshal Sir Harold Martin, KCB, DSO, DFC, AFC, is another description of the Aussie 'Micky' Martin, the legendary Dambuster, pronounced by Group Captain Leonard Cheshire, VC, DSO, DFC, as 'the greatest bomber pilot on the Allied side during the Second World War'. In 1974 the serving air marshal recalled:

I remember Sticky Murphy very well. I first met him when he was commanding No. 23 Squadron in February 1944 at Alghero in Sardinia. They were committed to intruder operations against

German aircraft operating from French and Italian airfields.

The circumstances of our meeting are these. I had been bombing from a base in Norfolk the Antheor Viaduct in the South of France, when my aircraft was hit. The bomb aimer was very badly wounded indeed. We subsequently discovered that he had been killed outright, but did not know this at the time. We therefore diverted ourselves to the nearest airfield in a state of some considerable emergency, but learned on the radio as we approached Alghero that there was no surgeon available, and we were advised to go to Cagliari in the south of Sardinia.

During the course of the night Sticky learned of our dilemma, and flew to Cagliari the following morning bearing money and all the other necessities of life for a crew stranded so far from its base.

After that sortie I was, on return to England, posted into intruders myself, and it was on No. 515 Squadron at Little Snoring, which came under No. 100 Group. To the best of my memory Sticky was killed fairly shortly afterwards, and I remember very much his operational aggressiveness, and gay positive style of leadership.

Wing Commander John Nesbitt-Dufort, DSO, Croix de Guerre – the officially recorded original, successful pick-up pilot – was pleased to recall:

Sticky Murphy tempered his skill with a very cheerful, happy-go-lucky attitude to operational flying, although to my knowledge he never took unnecessary chances, and was one of the most 'press-on' types I have known.

My confidence in him, his cheerful determination and guts, were confirmed on many occasions but notably when he flew home to Tangmere three hours after receiving a severe bullet wound in the neck when he was ambushed on the ground by the Germans on his first pick-up in a Lysander. Characteristically, although very weak with the loss of blood, on getting out of the bullet-torn aircraft with a broad grin, his first words were, 'Whoopee, John! I've been wounded!' He then gave a brief explanation of the events before walking unaided to the waiting ambulance.

It was not only the fact that Sticky Murphy picked me up in an Anson, extricating me from a very dangerous situation in France some months later, that made me mourn his death later in the war on operations. It was mainly that I had lost an extremely cheerful, gallant and close friend.

Alan Murphy was truly one of the most outstanding unsung heroes of the Second World War.

Air Commodore William Pitt-Brown, CBE, DFC, AFC, recalled in 1977:

Sticky Murphy was an outstanding man. He had an Austin Nippy two-seater and Dave Hanson had a Ford. Journeys in summer returning to Cranwell from the Newark swimming baths were fast, to say the least, especially on the Leadenham 'straight'.

One of the objects of Cranwell training was to make us 'all of a kind'. This instilled love of Service and a special kind of corporate discipline and bond between us. Sticky was a perfect example of the required end product.

At Cranwell he was a natural 'no bullshit' leader, well liked by everyone and highly proficient in his professional skills.

Squadron Leader Charles Price was the station intelligence officer at Little Snoring, and in constant touch with squadron commanders including Wing Commander Alan Murphy. In February 1975 he wrote:

Sticky was irrepressible, gay and lots of fun. But it wasn't all 'beer and skittles' with him. He played hard, but worked very hard. He was a very brave officer eager to get weaving, and help win the war.

Those of us who worked and lived with him during the war will never forget the devotion, affection and shining example of Wing Commander Murphy. That shall be his monument and reward. I am sure Sticky would subscribe to the following extract from Lord Samuel's memoirs: 'Death is not an injury, but rather like a privilege: and at the end we can be ready to rise cheerfully from the table as a grateful guest arises from an abundant feast.'

Flight Lieutenant Robert 'Jock' Reid flew continually with Sticky Murphy from the second week in June 1943 until late November 1944 as his navigator, involving over fifty operational sorties over France, Italy, Germany, Belgium and Holland. He recalled:

Socially Sticky was very much one for a party, whereas I had quieter tastes. He was proud of the fact that his identity card carried a description of the colour of his eyes as 'bloodshot blue'. He was a 'Pope Puff', the only one I ever met, indicating an outstanding capacity for carrying his drink.

Squadron Leader Micky Martin, who came to Little Snoring from the Dambusters, was of similar appearance, and I think his identity card carried the same description of the colour of his eyes.

With hindsight, and I have often thought about it, Sticky was a professional. His life was the Royal Air Force. He had been trained and disciplined to eliminate self from any action he took in combat. Most other airmen were civilians like myself, there only for the war. Our first thought was self-preservation, whereas with Sticky, performing the task in hand without thought of consequence to himself, was uppermost in his mind.

I think his wife, Jean, understood his attitude, and devotion to the Service. She asked me to take care of him and I understood what she meant and did my best. I think it was generally accepted that I acted as a brake on his impulsive nature, at least in the aircraft, and I grew to think that I was in a way responsible for keeping him out of trouble in the air.

Sticky used to call me 'Binder' – an RAF term meaning 'a constant grumbler' – and he was not without reason. The amount of tight rein I kept on him must surely have annoyed him, hence the nickname. It has been my lifelong regret that I was not available to fly with him to Gütersloh on that last trip. We were such an experienced team that I hope we would have survived.

Flight Lieutenant Bill Shattock, as he became, following Sticky's recommendation that all his NCO crews should be commissioned 'in the field', recollected:

Sticky Murphy was a man who led by example, never expected any of his crews to do more than he did himself. Because of his modesty his previous flying history was unknown to those who served with him on Mosquitoes.

He had the common touch, and was a buccaneer in the best sense of the word – unorthodox and daring, with a gaiety and panache which was not found among other leaders. He was quite extraordinary – outstanding as a man and operational pilot, and as a commander of a squadron traditionally composed of independent and self-reliant men. They reluctantly bowed their knee to any man. He was the one.

George Stewart of the Royal Canadian Air Force was only twenty-one when the war ended. He flew fifty sorties on No. 23 Squadron in a few months, and was known as 'Press On Regardless' and decorated with the Distinguished Flying Cross. During 1977 and 1978 he continued to fly exhibitions in Second World War aircraft in Canada and visited old squadron comrades with No. 23 Squadron flying Phantoms in England during 1978. He remembered:

Sticky was a firm leader when that was the issue, yet he had the capacity to romp like a youngster when a party was in progress. He had the 'no bullshit – let's do the job together' attitude of a front-line commander and I clearly remember seeing him at briefing when he would be scheduled for an operation, looking as casual and yet as eager as the rest of us.

I think it was only fitting that he chose his target on the last trip, one which we were all a bit nervous about, because it was the headquarters of the German night-fighter force – Gütersloh! We had lost Ken Eastwood on a trip there, and I flew with my navigator Paul Beaudet to Gütersloh on the next sortie after Sticky was lost.

I can still remember clearly the continuous sound of radar searching in my earphones throughout our intruding in German air-space. The area was sinister and foreboding, and I was pleased to return safely. Sticky was a fine leader and very much one of the guys. I remember him most vividly and his great sense of humour and love of life.

Flying Officer George Twitt reminisced in November 1974:

I was one of the band of six NCOs in Malta and elsewhere including Bill Shattock and Jim Coley, Shorty Dawson and Fergie Murray and my navigator John Irvin. Clearly I recall that uplift of morale with the arrival of Sticky Murphy as our fight commander in September 1943.

Later I served with him at Little Snoring, where I found him a sensitive and understanding squadron commander, aware of other people's problems, which was a new facet of his outstanding leadership.

The change from the Middle East band of 'Murphy's Marauders' to a more conventional RAF unit at Little Snoring added responsibilities which made Sticky more diplomatic, without lessening his panache and sense of fun, as well as his joy in living and taste for practical jokes. For example, he popped thunderflashes down the chimneys of huts and offices – shouting a warning, and roared with laughter at discomfiture. On one occasion he was taking a disciplinary hearing when the same thing happened to him, and there was a shout. The office emptied in confusion as the explosion occurred, but Sticky was unperturbed and resumed the 'trial' in a sooty atmosphere.

He was admired and respected by all the squadron, including the ground crews, who were made to feel very much a part of the squadron family, as they had been in the Middle East.

Still, after more than thirty years, I recall his gay personality and iron determination, operational example and leadership and his warm humanity. I have not since met his like.

Mrs Bessie Whitehead of Little Snoring, was the widow of a farmer, living on the edge of the aerodrome and still there in 1975 when she recollected:

I have such happy memories of Sticky Murphy and the other lads of the RAF station here. He had such natural charm, and used to come to the farmhouse in the evenings when they were not flying.

I will always remember the first night Sticky came here. In the early hours, when the lads had their jackets off and feet up on the mantle with large open fire, the door opened and my husband walked in.

'Come in old chap,' said Sticky with a wave, 'I don't know who you are, but come in and join the party.' They became good party chums after this.

Sticky lit up any company by his personality. He was a great tonic to us in those days, and shared a hut with Sammy Hoare built on our farm. Sticky took a pride in the garden there, with plants, shrubs and crazy paving.

Only once did I see Sticky exert any discipline over the lads, many of whom were from overseas and rather boisterous. Once they showed signs of having a rugby match, as if in their mess. Sticky quietly said, 'There will be none of that chaps. We are guests here.' They quietened down immediately, and had great respect for Sticky, in every way.

When Sticky first came to visit me – he had just to pop through the hedge to the house – he said, 'This is a real home where we can relax and talk about everything except the RAF.' I had a lovely kitchen garden, and he loved to change the seed tickets around, and was full of fun and mischief. Obviously he came from an outstanding family.

Sticky used to come into the kitchen when I was cooking, and say, 'This smells like home, Bess.' He asked when I was cooking again, and I told him. Once a week I had a good cook-up, and he used to bring currants, sugar, lard, margarine and butter from the mess, saying, 'Never mind how I get them.' I used to cook Norfolk shortcakes, and Sticky loved them, pinching them just out of the oven like a naughty schoolboy.

One of No. 23 Squadron's pilots, Duncan Sheriff, married my daughter, Sheila, and Buddy Badley was another favourite of ours. The squadron brought a good atmosphere with them, completely integrating with the people of the small village here, and had church parade each Sunday at the little local church. Sometimes Sticky used to read the lesson. One officer refused to take church parade and was posted away at once. Sammy Hoare was very religious.

Sticky remains vividly in my memory after more than thirty years have passed. He was a great loss to us all, and was missed by local people as much as by his comrades of the RAF.

Epilogue

Months of investigation in the 1970s traced Sticky Murphy's widow to the Isle of Wight, his sister to the Northamptonshire village of Barton Seagrave, his daughter to South Africa with her children, and other relatives, including cousin Pat Murphy, in Yorkshire. They were pleased, but surprised after thirty years, to find someone sharing their admiration of Alan Michael Murphy. All were generous with their time, and loan of research material, including his flying logbooks, photographs, documents and recollections. He remained fresh in memories, his sister having named her only son Michael. Sticky's photograph in uniform is prominently displayed at their family home, where close contact was maintained with the whole family. Surviving old comrades of Sticky, as well as schoolmasters, were traced and interviewed. Fresh facets of Sticky's character and personality at different stages of his life emerged. Two contemporary diaries were loaned, with many photographs and anecdotes.

In April 1974, on a trip to Sticky's grave at Oldebroek in the Netherlands with this author's son Peter, an inscription was found on the headstone: 'Known and loved by all who knew him as "Sticky".'

On the military lawn of honour stood a wide curve of official gravestones, the graves covered by tall, flowering shrubs and trees. Sticky's was flanked by those of Douglas Darbon and another RAF flight sergeant navigator, Donnel Entwistle. It was a poignant reminder to see that Sticky was only twenty-seven years old when killed. Three British soldiers and twenty airmen were accompanied there by three Canadian, one Australian, two New Zealand and one Czechoslovakian airmen. One New Zealander,

Sergeant Pine Tenga Takarangi (a wireless operator/air gunner) was a Maori from Putiki, and the Aussie, Pilot Officer Clive Henry Phillips, had parents in Mosman, New South Wales, and a wife in Hampstead, London.

Oldebroek was a small, sleepy farming community of warm hospitality, the graves being tended immaculately by successors of those who had buried Sticky and Douglas Darbon. A large hare scampered and bounced across the cemetery in the spring warmth, disturbing the tranquillity. Local people combined to express their admiration and respect for those who had died fighting Nazi oppression. Mynheer van Loo of Oldebroek went out of his way to supply documents and translations from local records about the fate of this No. 23 Squadron's crew.

Almost eighteen months later, the same team visited the Ardennes for a memorable meeting with Colonel Jean Cassart from Brussels, the agent for whom Sticky had been ambushed and wounded in December 1941. Colonel Cassart illustrated the events of the incident at Neufchâteau and related, modestly and reluctantly, his own history before, during and after the ambush, including his remarkable escape from Berlin.

A dinner party nearby, with his companions, reflected his continuing love of life and flair despite advancing years, and what a kindred spirit with Sticky he had. 'We were all dedicated,' he said truthfully, having heard previous stories of the ambuscade. Colonel Cassart looked forward to meeting his old friend John Nesbitt-Dufort, but this was not to be. A few days earlier, John had met Sticky's daughter, Mrs Gail Hanekom, on a visit to the Isle of Wight from South Africa. Later that day the author met her with Buddy Badley in the New Forest for a delightful chat. Gail had no memories of her father but appreciated a recording of his voice, photographs and a series of anecdotes illustrating his warmth and great personality.

A few days later, on 30 September 1975, John Nesbitt-Dufort died, following years of pain caused by the Lysander prang near Issoudun. At his funeral at Tunbridge Wells there were representatives of the SOE, Tempsford Society and No. 23 Squadron. If there is an afterlife, shades of many old comrades, including Sticky, welcomed another keen and energetic party man to their special Valhalla.

Another pilgrimage, with Bill Shattock to Malta in February 1976, found little change in the George Cross Island, except that it rained incessantly. At Sliema a block of flats comprised the former Balluta mess, of vile memory, and Meadowbank mess had become a modest hotel nearby. Young Maltese enthusiasts ran the Malta Model Aero Club, flying remote-controlled aircraft in formation take-offs and aerobatics, at Ta' Qali airstrip, now the recreation ground of the islanders. Luqa had become the main aerodrome, and there was little evidence of the old, battered wartime airfield. A tarmac runway made considerable difference from the old compressed lumps of local stone that Sticky and his pals had had to contend with.

The founder of the aero club was George Curmi, whose other claim to fame was a youthful flight with Wing Commander Peter Wykeham-Barnes in a Mosquito of No. 23 Squadron. With his son, Michael, George Curmi well remembered, as did others, the squadron that had reduced night raids with Mosquitoes, as Spitfires had eased daylight attacks.

Close touch had always been kept with Bill Shattock and John Irvin, then of Bridgwater and Crawley, respectively. Old comrades like Norman Conquer, David Atherton, George Twitt, Buddy Badley, Phil Russell, Jock Reid, Bill Gregory and Bruce Madge were gradually traced. Often enthusiastic historian Tommy Cushing, owner of Little Snoring airfield, had assisted. His childhood imagination had been fired by the Mosquitoes taking off over his home nearby. Air Chief Marshal Sir Lewis Hodges and Group Captain Ron Hockey of the Tempsford Society – the former at Cranwell with Sticky, and the latter in the early SOE days – kindly contributed their recollections, as did Captain Joe Cooper when visited in Jersey.

A meeting with Sticky's schoolmasters, Robin Graham and Yvone Kirkpatrick at Wimborne, near Canford School, proved interesting and instructive. Coincidental meetings took place with Wing Commander Freddy Lambert and John Austin, respectively CO of No. 515 Squadron at Little Snoring and another SOE pilot in the early days with Sticky.

Group Captain Brian Kingcome, a close Cranwell friend of Sticky, proved helpful, as did Mrs Bessie Whitehead, the farmer's wife at Little Snoring. Charles Bovill, a 'boffin' of SOE with Sticky and John Nesbitt-Dufort, became a friend, continuing with inventive work for long hours in 1978.

Douglas Higgins, squadron artist during 1942–45, painted Sticky's

Mosquito over at Little Snoring, as the aerodrome then was, for Tommy Cushing, and this received great praise. He had cheered the squadron crews with murals in the mess at Fertilia in Sardinia, and again at Little Snoring, being one of the longest-serving members of the ground staff on No. 23 Squadron. He had a tale to tell of Sticky's lack of petty stupidity, so prevalent among some senior Air Force officers of different mentality.

Kit Cotter was killed in a car accident in Holland while serving in the post-war forces in Germany, and Aussie Charlie Scherf met a similar fate in Australia. Wladislaw Rosycki died in Canada in 1970 and 'Baron' Goldie passed away as a Dorset farmer. Air Chief Marshal Sir Keith Park of Battle of Britain and Malta fame, the most loved of all the top leaders, died in New Zealand at the age of eighty-two. Douglas Darbon's father, Robert, was seen in Essex, and research revealed that Squadron Leader Alan Chalmers, who gave Sticky his nickname, died of wounds on active service. Wing Commander 'Teddy' Knowles perished in a Whitley accident, and Air Commodore 'Mouse' Fielden died in January 1977. Reg Adams, who flew on No. 23 in Malta and No. 515 at Little Snoring, passed away in October 1977.

A number of ex-No. 23 Squadron members and other linked to them remained in East Anglia, where the squadron was again based in 1977/78: Steve Ruffle of Sible Hedingham, who wrote a poem after a visit to Little Snoring; Mrs Rosemarie Lambert (née Swain, wife of Wing Commander Frederick Lambert) of Fakenham with her RAF tribute; Wykeham-Barnes's navigator in Malta, Flying Officer Palmer of Norwich; and, not least of all, Wing Commander Phil Russell, who came to live in retirement at Blakeney. All had lifelong memories of those days, as did David Porter, a former BBC executive who spared time from an international life to tell of his lucky escape from disaster in the Po Valley.

Flying over Norfolk with Tommy Cushing from Little Snoring on 26 July 1976 fired the imagination. There was the No. 23 Squadron dispersal in 1944/45. Into the mind came a picture of feverish activity as take-off time grew near: 'erks' preparing the aircraft, checking engines, electrics, radios, special radar equipment and airframes, and all under constant supervision and urging by NCOs to get it right. The coming and going of Service vans, fuel bowsers and bomb carriers; all the hustle concentrating on effective night sorties to shorten the war. Then came the crews, driven by WAAFs, who readily responded to nervous banter, but sometimes sobbed as aircraft rose into the night sky. They grieved in advance, unknown to aircrews.

Fergie Murray and Shorty Dawson had been killed on 21 March 1945 after helping to destroy the Gestapo headquarters at the Shell House, Copenhagen, liberating prisoners incarcerated and tortured. Veterans with No. 464 RAAF Squadron at this time, the raid was commemorated annually at the rebuilt Shell House by the Danes. Old comrades Irvin and Coley paid tribute to their memory on the thirty-second anniversary of the raid at that location, with survivors, and cast flowers into the sea where the crew perished, shot down by German cruisers.

Interesting meetings took place with legendary Danish Resistance heroes like General Tiemroth and Professor Mogens Fog, who escaped with others, and with Svend Truelsen, head of Danish military intelligence in 1944, working in conjunction with Air Vice Marshal Sir Basil Embry. Other former prisoners were Tage Hartmann-Schmidt (nicknamed 'Niki Lauda' during the visit), Bendt Nordentoft, Viktor Zohnesen, Ove Kampmann and Alf Ebbe Olstrup (secretary of the Prisoners' Society and organiser of the kindest reception and hospitality).

A Danish Tommy Cushing was found, named Ove Hermansen, who was researching all the Gestapo HQ strikes in Denmark by Mosquitoes. He, too, was most hospitable, and was connected with his Little Snoring counterpart, and with Aussies who had corresponded with the author about the Shell House raid, seeking concrete news of their friends' fate.

Finally, during the summer of 1978 there was a reunion of old comrades at No. 23 Squadron with their Phantoms at Wattisham, still doing their stuff, despite successive governments, in the 1938 style. Sixteen 'old codgers' met, many not having done so for more than thirty years. Added to those previously named were Harry Heath, John Rivaz and Morris Spender. George Stewart came from Canada, Jock Reid from Scotland, and Ted Ryciak ('Ritzy') after twenty-six years in Zambia. Sticky Murphy and other absent friends were not forgotten in the reminiscences.

The Greeks said that a man is immortal if his name is recalled among men.

Wing Commander Nesbitt-Dufort on flying Lysanders on 'pimpernel' missions

In 1974, John Nesbitt-Dufort gave an account of his experiences of Special Operations Executive pick-ups (known as 'pimpernel' missions) over enemy territory:

Towards the end of 1941, no less than five night pick-up operations had been successfully completed and the two British organisations employing secret agents, i.e. 'C' and 'SOE' – the Foreign Office and Special Operations Executive – were not slow to appreciate the advantages of this convenient method of conveying their 'Joes' to and from their dangerous work in the 'field' – as they described their theatre of operations.

This led to the organisations demanding more pick-up operations during the full moon period than I could possibly cope with. As a result, permission was granted to increase the establishment of the flight in No. 138 Squadron, which had superseded No. 1419 Flight, from three Lysanders to four by the addition of another operational machine. A French pilot, Flight Lieutenant St Laurent, was posted to my flight but unhappily crashed on a non-operational flight within a few days of arriving, writing off the Lysander and killing not only himself but a passenger who was one of the best fitters on this type of aircraft.

The first training aircraft, Lysander R2626, was then brought back into service and T.1508 made operational, giving two trainers and two operational aircraft. The crew establishment was raised to three and

I was given permission to select my own pilots.

On hearing about this, Flight Lieutenant Sticky Murphy and Flying Officer Guy Lockhart immediately volunteered. Both were promoted shortly afterwards and each was a very experienced pilot.

Whereas Guy – an ex-Spitfire pilot who had escaped from the notorious Miranda Spanish internment camp after being shot down – was rather intense, Sticky tempered his skill with a very cheerful, happy-go-lucky attitude to operational flying. To my knowledge, he never took unnecessary chances, yet was one of the most 'press-on' types I have known.

Neither pilot needed any encouragement to pile up the necessary flying hours to get thoroughly familiar with the docile Lysander and the unusual flap arrangement. In a couple of weeks both of them were completely at home in the machine and putting down super-short stoppers at night.

The next part of their training was simplicity itself. The obvious way to teach them pick-up procedure was to tell them everything I knew about it myself, then allocate each a couple of agents who were due to go into the 'field' shortly, for them to train them themselves. When the time came for the agents to return to the country, Guy and Sticky were to do the actual pick-up operations of their own trainees, so that if anything went wrong with the procedure, they could only blame themselves.

Having briefed the pilots as thoroughly as I could, I supervised the training with an agent for a couple of nights before I had to go down to the special SOE School at Beaulieu to give lectures to classes of agents 'en masse' as a preliminary to their flying procedure training. On my return after about ten days I found that Sticky had entered into the spirit of the game with his usual cheerful enthusiasm and had made excellent progress.

Obviously I could teach him nothing about aerial navigation at night, as he had been flying as captain of his own Whitley after a period of flying with Wing Commander Teddy Knowles, the squadron commander, on agent parachute-dropping sorties in Whitleys.

I could give him a few useful tips on agent pick-up training, which went as follows:

The agent was taken out during the hours of daylight by his pilot in a car, generally driven by a FANY driver. While being driven through the countryside, Sticky would ask his training agent to select a field which was in his opinion large enough for a Lysander to land in and take off again comfortably in the dark. This sounds pretty simple but it was surprising what completely unsuitable small fields agents – who had no pilot experience – considered adequate when first presented with this choice. In addition, the approaches had to be good and all exits clear of obstructions. The field had to be level, and the surface not too rough or too soft after rain. (Aircraft were to get bogged down after more than one subsequent pick-up.)

Having satisfied Sticky on all the above points and selected a field, the agent was taught how to make an accurate map reference of the field, which he handed to his instructor.

The agent would then be shown how to lay a miniature flarepath and made to do it himself dead in the wind to Sticky's satisfaction.

Back at base the agent was shown how to embark and disembark, put on the unfamiliar observer-type parachute harness and the use of the intercom. He was also told to listen carefully to the sound of a circling Lysander's engine and memorise the note. He was also taught how to signal with a powerful torch an agreed Morse letter of recognition to be kept secret, to bring the pilot in to land after hearing the two distinct bursts of engine from the Lysander pilot in acknowledgement of his signal.

Later, not necessarily when there was a moon, the agent would be driven out to his field by himself at night and lay out his unlit flarepath in plenty of time before his agreed practice pick-up time, and wait at No. 1 torch for Sticky's arrival.

Sticky would then take off from base and fly to the field, circling it at about 500 feet. Immediately on recognising the sound of the Lysander the agent would sprint around lighting his torches and then signal the aircraft in. After touchdown the agent had to rush around collecting his torches (No. 1 last) before embarking and Sticky would take off after a quick glance at his stopwatch.

He might, if the field was suitable, land back in the field again without a flarepath, disembark his agent and the whole procedure was practised again and again until Sticky was absolutely satisfied with the efficiency and speed of the agent. Normally four minutes was considered adequate from touchdown to take-off.

Personally I never had any qualms about Sticky's ability to cope with any unforeseen snags. This confidence in him, his cheerful determination and guts, were confirmed on many occasions.

The 'Lizzie' as all marks of the Lysander were affectionately known in the RAF, were single-engined, two-/three-seater, semi-cantilever, high mid-wing-braced monoplanes. With spatted landing wheels, a carrot-shaped fuselage, sensitive ailerons, elevators with a larger surface than a tailplane, almost dainty dragonfly-like wings and adequate power, the Lysander was fast and extremely manoeuvrable, the latter virtue also applying at very low speeds.

Although originally entering the Service in 1938 for Army cooperation duties, it was virtually the first short take-off and land type of aircraft in use by the Allies in the Second World War. Soon it was found to be ideally suited to the secret agent pick-up type of operation. Needless to say, its delightful handling qualities, coupled with a very useful turn of speed, endeared it to the pilots who flew these planes on this kind of work.

On one's initial flight in the Lysander, the first thing that had to be mastered was the unorthodox method of flap operation. The HP Autoslots which extended the whole length of the leading edges of the wings were coupled directly to the trailing edge flaps. At first this arrangement could be a little disconcerting, as when approaching to land, on reducing the speed to just below 80mph the slots opened, and this automatically lowered the flaps, necessitating the application of a little backward trim. On take-off the procedure was of course reversed, but the pilot soon got used to this, and instinctively trimmed and kept either well above or below the slot operating speed as conditions demanded.

In the air the Lysander was intrinsically stable and by careful adjustment of elevator and rudder trims, could be flown hands off – a valuable asset to the pilot/navigator. With a top speed in the neighbourhood of 230mph, it was in fact faster than some of the single-seater fighters in service at the time of conception, and a useful 180mph cruising speed could be comfortably maintained.

As STOL [short take-off and landing] aircraft they could be landed and taken off in comparatively small fields, provided of course that the surface was reasonably firm and smooth. At normal approach speed of about 65mph, a landing run of only 150 yards, with even moderate use of the brakes, was easily attainable. In a stiffish wind I have personally achieved a take-off – with the use of the automatic boost control cut out – in thirty-six yards. Level flight (admittedly at well under maximum carrying capacity) has been maintained at below 55mph, and at 60mph a steep angle of approach over obstacles presented no difficulty. A very spectacular short landing run was also obtainable by the experienced pilot by reducing the airspeed down to just over 50mph and holding the stick firmly back while the engine was given plenty of throttle, the aircraft then descending practically vertically like a lift and running virtually only a few yards after touchdown.

The last manoeuvre was really only a demonstration stunt, as at not less than twenty-five feet, almost full throttle had to be applied and the stick eased forward at the same time. This type of landing required considerable skill on the part of the pilot; faulty judgement of height and timing could, and sometimes did – when attempted by the inexperienced – result in the undercarriage doing the splits to the accompaniment of very expensive noises.

The aircraft was easy to fly, had no vices whatsoever, and was very forgiving, provided of course that one made no absurd demands upon the machine. Stall and recovery were normal, and the sensible positioning of the adjustable landing lights in the spats made accurate night landings extremely easy, as the pilot could see his exact height right down to a few inches above the ground.

The cockpit was comfortable and roomy with an excellent view

down and ahead, although somewhat restricted aft. The only
discomfort suffered by the pilot was due to long hours sitting on the
hard dinghy pack on his seat-type parachute, but this could hardly be
blamed on the aircraft.

Before being used for pick-up operations, the Lysander was
extensively modified. Firstly, all offensive and defensive armaments
were removed, the former consisting of detachable stub wings
carrying small bomb racks, and twin unsynchronised .303 Browning
machine guns were mounted outboard and inboard respectively of
the spats. Defensive armament was merely a single free-mounted
.303 Vickers K (gas-operated) machine gun in the aft cockpit and
armour plating behind the pilot's back.

This considerable lightening of the aircraft not only permitted
the carrying of extra fuel in a special long-range petrol tank slung
externally below the belly of the aircraft, but in addition provided
extra room for a third person in the rear.

A short ladder, to permit easy and rapid exit and entrance, was
permanently fixed to the outside of the fuselage on the port side, just
below the rear cockpit. The whole aircraft was then given an overall
coat of matt black paint and the modifications were complete.
The following additional details concerning the Lysander Mk III
might be relevant or of interest. The power plant was one single-row,
air-cooled radial Bristol Mercury XXX medium supercharged engine
of 870hp. It drove a two-pitch, three-bladed airscrew. The maximum
AUW [all-up weight] was 10,000lb and the endurance (with a long-
range tank) approximately eight hours. The wingspan was fifty feet,
length thirty feet six inches, and height fourteen feet six inches. This
really magnificent aeroplane flew more than 400 operational sorties
with the two Special Duty Squadrons.

John Nesbitt-Dufort expanded his account with his know-how on pilot
navigation in Lysanders at night:

In view of the inherent stability of the Lysander, pilot navigation
during the full-moon period at night, in good visibility to and from a
pick-up rendezvous, normally presented no problems, but in turbulent

cloud and poor visibility, to which was often added the complication
of avoiding enemy flak, night fighters or searchlights, the pilot
would then find his hands full. Thus on deep-penetration operations,
flights over seven hours' duration were sometimes made; a
combination of poor weather and enemy harassment could prove
very exhausting.

Detailed and meticulous flight planning was absolutely necessary
immediately prior to every sortie, operational altitude winds being
taken from last-minute forecasts.

A few days before the date of any anticipated pick-up operation,
the field that had been selected by the agent for the landing, in more
than one instance a disused airfield, was photographed from the air;
this was done by a high-flying Spitfire from a PRU [Photographic
Reconnaissance Unit]. This photograph was then submitted to the
pilot concerned for acceptance as to size and suitability with regards
to the surrounding obstacles etc. If these were acceptable to the pilot,
he would agree to the field and he was then committed to the landing.
He would then scrutinise it further for easily identifiable landmarks
on the adjacent countryside, as this photograph, an ETA and a four-
figure Michelin guide map reference would be all the information the
pilot had as to his destination. Radio silence was naturally maintained
except in the immediate vicinity of his home base, generally
Tangmere.

On the morning prior to the night operation, the pilot would fly
down from his permanent base, either Newmarket or Tempsford to
Tangmere, treating this flight as a night flying test. On arrival there
he would supervise the refuelling and correction of any engine, radio
or airframe snags encountered on the way down. He would then check
his tracks and distances, which would give him also an approximate
estimated time of departure [ETD].

The afternoon was usually taken up with sleep, and in the evening
after a good meal a thorough meteorological briefing was available.
Unless the weather forecast earlier had been impossible, a confirmation
that the operation was on had been sent, via the six o'clock news on
the Foreign Service of the BBC, to the agent.

The pilot then, with the most recent and accurate information as to forecast visibility, cloud cover and winds at the relevant altitudes, worked out his courses, grounds speeds and resulting ETAs at the various turning points and landmarks. Normally he used a 1:50,000-scale air navigation map for the whole trip except for the last few miles, for which he would revert to a quarter-inch-scale map.

His outgoing passenger, if any, would arrive by car with an escorting officer in plenty of time to be briefed again on disembarkation procedure. Take-off was generally made at ETD minus ten minutes to allow for unexpected trouble in the shape of enemy interference or, more often, inaccuracies in wind forecast. Power and speed could always be reduced on the last leg if necessary, but trying to make up time could be expensive on precious fuel.

[The pilot's] first course on climb-out over the Channel might be deliberately twenty-five degrees off that required to reach his point of entry on the French coast, and on attaining cruising altitude – generally 14,000 feet – he was allowed a single VHF back-bearing. This would allow him to check his drift and adjust his new course if necessary. It also gave the Germans, who monitored all VHF transmissions, a false idea of his actual track and subsequent point of entry. Radio silence would now have to be observed until fifteen minutes out on the return journey, when a homing bearing would be available if required.

From now on, over the sea, an extremely accurate course and airspeed had to be maintained in order to hit that initial vitally important pinpoint over the enemy coast, usually a well-defined landmark. At the first sign of searchlights and flak, when weaving became imperative, he would be careful to weave the same number of degrees in either direction in order to maintain his mean course; as can be understood, there was little future wandering up and down the enemy coast while trying to establish one's exact position.

Having pinpointed himself and shaken off enemy attention, sometimes by a fast-diving corkscrew, the pilot would settle down on his new course at just over 6,000 feet (out of the range of light flak) and carry out the usual check for drift at his next important landmark, adjustments in course being made as necessary. In clear moonlight conditions with no enemy interference this was much easier than it sounds, and on approaching the target area the pilot switched to his quarter-inch map and simply map-read himself to the field where the agent was waiting.

On hearing the Lysander's engine the agent would lay out a miniature flarepath of three torches shining downwind; these were placed in the form of an inverted letter 'L', the dimensions of which were 150 yards and 50 yards. The agent would then flash an agreed Morse letter on a more powerful torch at the aircraft, and the pilot would acknowledge this by two distinct bursts of engine, and land to the right of the flarepath. He touched down as near to the first torch as possible, running between two torches at the top, taxiing back to the first torch again before turning into wind. As he was taxiing back, the agent or his 'helper' would sprint round after him collecting the top two torches before returning to collect the first torch at which the Lysander was now waiting. Disembarkation of the outgoing agent and embarkation of the one to be brought home then took place, and the pilot took off without a flarepath on his DI [Direction Indicator] heading, nearly always using his automatic boost cut-out for an extra short run.

Navigation home was merely a reverse of the outgoing procedure, but on approaching the coast again extra care had to be taken to avoid the already alerted standing German night-fighter patrols, and often a different route home was used to avoid them.

As soon as the pilot was safely near enough to base to do so, radio silence could be broken and welcome VHF QDMs (courses to steer to base) obtained. In the event of radio failure, searchlight homings were available.

Colonel Jean Cassart – 'Neufchâteau Ambush' and sequel

In 1975, Colonel Jean Cassart gave his recollections of the events at Neufchâteau, and subsequently when he was codenamed 'Capitaine Métrat':

I first made the acquaintance of Flight Lieutenant John Nesbitt-Dufort of the Royal Air Force on 17 July 1941. I introduced myself to him and gradually little by little told him of my trials, which had already been an adventure story.

How and why a Belgian (and almost a fanatic at that young age) I had always had the feeling of sympathy more towards England than the other neighbouring countries which I had more frequently visited.

How I had had this presentiment of war in 1933, and how with the years I saw it become increasingly more inevitable and always more imminent, and how finally, by a strange combination of circumstances, I was surprised on 10 May 1940 in the morning to be woken up by the sound of a bombardment.

How on 28 May 1940, after the surrender of the Belgian Army, I had escaped ingloriously having already had the experience of a first escape a week previously when I found myself by an error of judgement surrounded by German armoured troops who despised me and took no notice of me.

I told him how I had wandered for months in Belgium, in France and in Switzerland, then wasting two months in Algeria and Morocco and finally a month in Portugal, before managing to get to London.

It was decided that I should return to Belgium, on first retracing my journey the other way round in view of the contacts which I had made in the course of my travels, but then this plan was changed to returning me quickly by parachute, if I accepted the invitation to jump.

I was pleased to accept this invitation, discreetly forgetting to tell them that I had already three fractures of my spine and it was only two years since I had had a good deal of trouble with my right ankle.

That meant a return sleeping compartment to Ringway where I qualified as a parachutist after thirty minutes' training.

It was then decided that I should be freed from the task of making radio transmissions and that I should not myself do this work but would be accompanied by a radio operator. I was pleased to accept this on condition that I could choose my own operator and it was in this way that the completely devoted young Sergeant Henri Verhagen accompanied me and became a real friend.

All this had taken plenty of time and I was hoping to leave on the next full moon. Finally it was decided to avoid the uncertainty of my return journey; the best way was to go back by Lysander and I then followed the training to accomplish this and I met with Flight Lieutenant Dufort who was eventually to come to Belgium and recover me.

On Thursday 17 July 1941 at 11.30am I took the train to Brockenhurst where Flight Lieutenant Dufort was waiting for me at the station and took me to Beaulieu where there was a house which gave us a great welcome.

We passed the afternoon chatting and I saw a photograph of the aircraft and learned that it would be necessary to place certain lights on the ground and that the way in which to get into the plane was quite a climb.

We talked also of sports and I admitted that I had never played golf. Flight Lieutenant Dufort offered to initiate me and I accepted this offer with pleasure and that's what happened. It was necessary to take up this particular position, hold the club in this way, hit the ball like this and … woof! I was quite satisfied to have made contact with the ball but this object took upon itself to land about fifty centimetres from the hole. The people congratulated me but they had a funny look on their faces and I understood later that my claim that I had never played the game before appeared to be a joke and that this was a joke in rather bad taste. Unfortunately my later efforts which followed gave no doubt that I had not been joking but was serious in what I had said.

The next day, Friday afternoon, we flew in the Lysander; that is to say, I found how to get into the aeroplane quickly, what to do on board and what to do when we landed, so that I could get out in a few seconds. Flight Lieutenant Dufort said that he was satisfied and that the next flight would be at night the following day. [But] bad weather prevented this flight on the Friday evening and we spent the evening in Southampton with the best dinner available.

On the Sunday afternoon I expressed a strange interest in the stones of Stonehenge and Flight Lieutenant Dufort was willing to take me there and show me around. I remain grateful to him because it must have appeared to him a whim of the moment but, nevertheless, after more than thirty years I would like to go back there again.

When it came to the night flight, I put the lights out correctly, got in very quickly, and the next evening we had another night flight without us talking about it in advance and Lieutenant Dufort seemed satisfied with my progress.

The following Monday, 21 July (our National Feast Day in Belgium), weather prevented any flying and the only thing we did during the day was to confirm that I was a very poor golfer.

On Tuesday the 22nd, we lunched in Bournemouth and in the evening a performance of the lights, signals, take-off, taxi, landing, unloading and all that business went off correctly. Lieutenant Dufort was satisfied. There was between us a very strict arrangement. One letter of the alphabet was to serve as a code between we two and we two only.

When he had seen the spot where he was to land, seen the three lights marking the point of landing and the red one marking the point where he was to come back and pick up passengers, it was agreed that he would only land on a signal from me with a white light from a position close to the red lamp flashing in Morse the agreed letter. He asked me to tell nobody, that goes without saying, but also not to write down the letter which would have to do, but on the other hand the letter that I chose had to be chosen on the basis that there was no possible chance of me forgetting it. I chose the letter 'L', the initial of my king [Leopold III].

On Wednesday 23 July I said goodbye. I had only come for a few days and I was still in a ridiculous hurry but I had had plenty of time to learn to get into the plane; in fact ten minutes might have been sufficient in order to get into the aircraft once and remember it perhaps, but to know each other properly that would not have been enough. I left Lieutenant Dufort regretfully; 'Don't forget your letter!' 'Never fear!'

We had got on very well. We looked forward to meeting again on the other side in about three months. We knew at the same time that it would be a very unusual time to go through together, but I trusted him. I hoped that I inspired the same feeling in him.

After two nights of flying in vain over the Ardennes at low altitude but always in cloud, at last – on the night of 26/27 August by moonlight – we were parachuted, Henri and I, 'blind' but right in the middle of the Ardennes at a few hundred metres from the place we wanted to be. Almost home in fact, thanks to another pilot in the RAF whom I shall never know.

As soon as we were in Belgium the two main problems which we were posed soon made life harassing, and at the beginning I neglected to some extent the problem of my return to England.

Luckily some airman friends were willing to take on the job of finding the runways which would be suitable for the Lysander. The first that were found were too far to the west of Belgium and in the region of the German anti-aircraft defences, and these were refused. At the end of November a landing ground at the end of Neufchâteau, which had been used by the Luftwaffe in 1940, was found suitable, thank goodness. Because too many radio transmissions were not advisable and the moon was already nearly full, there were only a few possible nights and a settlement of the date through messages by the BBC was a good idea. From 8 December onwards the message 'The Éburons will come back' would signal that the date was put off until the next day, whereas the message 'The Ménapiens are very powerful' meant that Lieutenant Dufort had set out that very day.

On 8 December at 7.15pm we heard the message we were hoping
for. Long live the Ménapiens!

We were dug in at Vonêche near Beauraing where we were awaiting
a parachute drop of supplies. Henri had brought his radio apparatus
and I two cases of documents which I proposed to take to London.
At about fifty kilometres from Neufchâteau where John took us in his
car, we thought that we were ready for any eventuality. At the time of
receiving the message from the BBC we left, but had difficulty with ice
on the roads and arrived at Neufchâteau only a few minutes before
eleven o'clock, which was the time we were to wait from.

It was all white with snow and very misty. We tucked away the car
in a little road which we knew of and set out carrying the two cases
and three torches for the place we were to be picked up [from], and
we set out there the red lamp. John went back to the car to find something, while Henri and I were placing the two white lamps as agreed
at 100 and 150 metres from the direction facing the wind.

When we got back to the red lamp, Henri suddenly stopped me,
saying: 'I hear someone talking.' The moon was beginning to rise and
we thought we could pick out shadows. Were they soldiers or country
people? We wanted to know which they were and I cocked my pistol
and walked towards the shadows. After three steps Henri stopped me
again, saying: 'Hang on a minute, I can see five shadows and we are
only two. I think I can see some helmets as well.' Suddenly (in
German) – 'Halt, who goes there?'

I shouted to Henri, 'Run!' He made a half turn and I ran off squarely
to his left and toward a slope. Immediately there was a fusillade of
shots and howlings in German! I was wounded in the left arm just at
the height of my heart, but I went down the slope through some small
fields surrounded by wire, got under the wire by rolling underneath
without catching up on it!

At the bottom end of the slope, across a stream, I slipped. I
stumbled into the freezing water and lost my pistol. I climbed the
bank on the opposite side but found this very painful. I was panting
and tried to get towards a dark shadow which I thought would be a
wood. Going up the opposite slope I thought I was going to get to the

top when suddenly there was a cry: 'Halt!' I threw myself to the left
and was shot at twice more. I wanted to run but I couldn't run any
further. I dragged myself through the bushes that separated me from a
wall, which was that of Neufchâteau Cemetery.

While I was trying to get through an enclosure to get into a
meadow beyond, I saw there some German soldiers and behind me
the noise was getting closer. I slid down in the snow and the bushes at
the foot of the wall and crouched down.

Five soldiers were following me, looking with torches for my foot-
prints in the snow. When they got to the field they talked it over
among themselves with other soldiers who had come from another
meadow, who confirmed that they had seen nothing at all. There were
about ten of them in all, with space between them and me of about
one and a half to five metres, and they all had very strong torches like
searchlights. All was lost!

Me in my black coat in the fresh white snow; I did not move
because I was too exhausted. I distinctly heard the words, 'This track
is probably an old one', and they went off, strolling away. One last one,
a few metres from me, trained his light right on me, keeping it on me
and seemed to be looking … but then he too went away.

I was abandoned there, in a black coat, behind three clumps of
bushes which had no leaves on them, in the snow and in the
moonlight. I did not try to understand why, but just tried to get my
breath back. It was very uncomfortable lying there in all sorts of old
iron rubbish and old tins, but it seemed to me that the slightest
movement that I made created an awful noise. I saw the soldiers on
the right and on the left. There was now a volley of shots on the hill
in front of me, on the side perhaps where John had gone? No, for
alerted by the first volley, he had made himself scarce and went back
to his car which he found surrounded by soldiers. He walked all night
and found his way back to Vonêche.

Then the direction of Henri? It was he who was captured, and
managed to escape again.

What about Lieutenant Dufort? The problem was very different
[for him]. He was certainly free and I did not fear for him … not yet!
Since I had left him, how many times had I thought about his difficulty

of coming over from England [and] finding three poor little lights
[that] were rammed into the heart of the wild Ardennes countryside;
I couldn't help being very anxious on one point – would he find the
lights? I know by experience that it is not easy, but I had the greatest
confidence and remained optimistic. Lieutenant Dufort would find
the lights! All at once I had a change of opinion. It was really very
difficult, almost a gamble! Lieutenant Dufort would not find the lights
and I couldn't ignore the fact that although they were placed in their
boxes they could have been covered up and hidden. No, he wouldn't
find them. …

Heaven, I hope he didn't find them! … Brrr … what was that? …
Brrr … without doubt it was the sound of an engine. … It was an
aeroplane. … It was him! He came from the west at the height of a few
hundred feet, but turned through 180 degrees, reducing height, and
flew over the landing ground and gave his signal of several bursts of
engine. Without doubt the lights were correctly placed, were lit, and
Lieutenant Dufort had seen them! Up till then everything happened
so quickly that I had not been afraid, but now I trembled. It was silly
to worry because the letter 'L' which was agreed upon had not been
sent. I was the only person who knew it – even Henri my radio operator
who had come with me, did not know what the code letter was to be
signalled to the aircraft.

It was silly to tremble, but I trembled. At the same time up above,
Lieutenant Dufort was circling and swooping over the landing ground
at much lower altitude and giving further bursts of engine as a signal.
On the opposite side of the valley I could see him circling as if to say
he was coming in very quickly. But again Lieutenant Dufort crossed
almost at ground level with his landing lights on! He must be asking
himself why the agreed letter had not been flashed in Morse. It was an
unusual happening was it not? He had illuminated the landing ground
and seen nothing. … He decided to land – and to become a victim of
his too general zeal.

From my 'observatory' I saw and heard all this going on, and some
further bursts of the engine: was he going to land just the same? And
would he get to the pick-up point? But yet, he had landed and the engine
had slowed down and was coming to a stop right by the red lamp.

But immediately there were loud shouts from all the soldiers who came out of the wood, and at the same time a loud cracking noise [was heard]. Lieutenant Dufort must have been well on his guard as he had probably never taken off so quickly and in such a short distance. He turned to the left and passed right over my head without suspecting my feelings as I was struggling only a few tens of metres below him. Ouf!

Before he landed I was well aware of the dangers and it appeared silly to me that he should land without having had my agreed signal. When I realised that the landing had taken place I was amazed. Now that he had escaped I told myself that perhaps he had thought of the bad golf player, the strange enthusiast of ancient stones, of his companion in arms, and had risked his life rather than leave [me and the others] in the lurch.

But how could they ever thank him? I dreamed often about this, but when I found out how he had gone back to England ['he' actually being pilot Sticky Murphy and not John Nesbitt-Dufort, who had been grounded due to illness, a situation unknown to Jean Cassart at the time], he the fourth escaper of the four participants in the events at Neufchâteau, I learned also that I would never see him again and could only keep these thoughts in my memory.

After, I was left lying in the snow, shot in the left arm; I awoke in the early light to find a local man looking down at me and saying: 'You must have been very cold there.' He was standing on the edge of the cemetery, which overlooked the landing ground and woods where the events of the previous night had taken place.

I asked him if there were any Boche and he said that the town was full of them, but not in the immediate vicinity. Surprised and even afraid I looked around to the places where I had seen soldiers during the night – absolutely nobody. I jumped over the wall into the cemetery; nobody, the man had gone.

I crossed the cemetery and walked into Neufchâteau. I met a local priest who directed me to the local librarian who was a good patriot. I saw this man, who helped me with money and assisted me in my frozen and shocked state, as a result of which I got to Liège and then to Brussels. I made contact with my comrades of the Resistance there and a message was sent to SOE headquarters in London, congratulating the pilot for his brave attempt at rescue, and hoping that he had not been wounded and was safe.

We did not then know that we had been betrayed by a man who had infiltrated our circle and that this was the cause of the ambush, but shortly afterwards the Germans captured me. This was the result of a further betrayal by the same person. He was tried after the war in Belgium and shot for his treachery.

As a prisoner of the Germans for twenty-two months, I was tortured frequently in an effort to find out information which I would not disclose and was starved and kept in solitary confinement for long periods. In various prisons the treatment was the same, but although I was willing to talk about myself, I was unwilling to talk about my duties or comrades and had a variety of interrogators.

On one occasion my monocle was produced to me by a German officer who held it in his hand and asked what it was. I took it, fitted it into place in my right eye immediately, saying: 'C'est mon monocle!' He was convinced it had no sinister meaning and treated me with more respect after this. I could not have been treated with less respect before this.

Finally I was moved to a central prison in Berlin, where I was treated much better. A general interrogated me, at first asking questions only about myself which I answered freely. However, after an hour the questions meandered and finally focused on information about my activities and comrades, which I refused to give. The general, still calm in his manner, said that he would send me to prison for a further two weeks, in order that I could reconsider the situation, which was becoming a bit monotonous by now.

After five weeks I was again sent for and questioned, and the general tried to reason with me, pointing out that I was an intelligent man and that I would know what was best for me in the circumstances. I could only apologise and was sent back to prison again for two months or so to reconsider. After this period I was again called for and this time asked only one question: 'Have you changed your mind?' I answered in the negative. The general, still very polite, translated my answer on his way to his secretary, dictating, 'Ich habe

keine Antwort zu geben. Ich will keinen Verräter sein!' I was asked to
sign and I did. In English it meant: 'I have no answer to give. I will not
be a traitor.'

Some time after this there was a tribunal in Berlin at which
seventeen of us were tried and numbered one to seventeen. I was
number one. There was a general, Judge President and four colonels
sitting together.

The general started with me, asking if I knew the decision of
General von Falkenhausen, number so and so, from 10 May 1940,
saying it was not allowed to carry weapons in Belgium, and I had been
arrested with a pistol in my pocket. I must confess that I did not know
the decision, but that I found it so normal that I agreed to consider
just as if I had known it, and … I was sentenced to death! For other
charges I was sentenced again, every time to death, and altogether
seven times, rather funny because seven is my lucky number.

Number two did not defend himself and was quickly also sentenced
to death. Number three, Mr Dockx, defended himself very strongly
and denied different accusations, so that the President asked for the
deposition of a witness who we did not know at all. This man declared
he had been present at a certain meeting between Mr Dockx and other
prisoners. We were all astonished, but Mr Dockx was so indignant
that he did not say to the President but to me: 'Jean it's false. I have
never seen this man!' Unfortunately he had always denied knowing
me. We all felt the mistake and that Mr Dockx and his defence were
lost. The situation was very confused and the President decided to
carry on with one prisoner only at a time.

We were in one room together, and there was only one guard, all
the others staying in the court for the proceedings. Our guard had
become quite well known to us as he had been with us for four days
during the trial. Several of us asked if we could go to the toilet and
he let four of us go, including me, presumably not thinking that an
escape was possible from this well-guarded building.

In the toilet I said to the other prisoners that this was an ideal time
to try and escape, but they were demoralised and refused to make the
attempt. I apologised to them and said that I would try, and put on a
pair of spectacles and cap which I had found left by a civilian work-

man. Calmly and slowly I sauntered out of the building and on the way walked over a newly polished floor and was screamed at by a cleaning woman. I could hardly believe my eyes as I approached the main exit of the building. There were five guards, four of whom appeared to be off duty, but one was definitely on watch for persons leaving. As he appeared to be going to challenge me I walked straight up to him and just as he began to open his mouth I saluted with the Nazi salute, and said, 'Heil Hitler'. I kept on walking.

Suddenly, to my surprise, I was free in the street. I had a vague idea of the geography of Berlin and did not hurry but mingled with the crowd until that evening when I came across a young couple speaking French. I told them that I was called 'Capitaine Bernard', needed help and was thirsty. The girl was apprehensive and the man gave me money for a drink. I was having a drink in a local bar when two German policemen entered and sat down close to me. I was anxious, but they were obviously there just for a drink. I promptly left.

I soon found that the main railway stations were well guarded by the Germans, and after walking forty-four kilometres the first day and ten kilometres the next day, I was absolutely exhausted after my long spell in prison. I hoped to head for Switzerland, but I came across a working party of Frenchmen, and confided in them. They were cooperative and collected some money for me. They said that they had permission to travel within fifty kilometres of their working address. Also they said that local trains were never checked, and it was therefore possible to travel in a series of short trips. They also gave me food and encouragement. By using a series of trains, and especially seven on the final day, I made my way to Belgium and contact with the Resistance once more.

It had taken me only a few days to reach my homeland and within another twelve days, conveyed through the escape route for Allied airmen and others, I reached Gibraltar and then the United Kingdom. On arrival there I disclosed my escape from Berlin and other adventures and was immediately locked up for two months while they investigated my story. Finally I was cleared of any suspicion and was given command of a Special Air Service unit of parachutist saboteurs, and was again dropped into Belgium as the invasion force advanced.

Later I heard that all but myself and one other man of the seventeen had been executed, and that the Germans searched the building until after midnight, the guards having sworn that no person has passed them without a hat. During my escape I noted 'Wanted' posters out for me, but not for a man with a hat and spectacles. During the Second World War I used many aliases.

Translation of German Army report of 'Neufchâteau Ambush' and abortive efforts to capture Sticky Murphy and Jean Cassart

Field Command (V) 682, Namur 9.12.41
K Section Ia

To: Military Commander in Belgium and Northern France
Command staff Ia

Brussels
Re: daily report (*encl: 1*)

1. *Alterations in details*
a. units attached to Field Command (V) 682 – none
b. units not attached to Field Command (V) 682 – none

2. *Special matters*
(a) enemy flight action   none
(b) espionage cases   none
(c) sabotage cases   none
(d) accident cases   none
(e) mood and conduct of population   unchanged
(f) others: in the night of 8 till 9 December, an English aircraft landed on the disused airstrip near Neufchateau [sic]. In connection herewith, 2 suitcases – one of which contained message material – were taken from Belgian civilians. Detailed report enclosed.

(g) losses   none

The Field Commander
Signed: von Walther
Colonel
pp [illegible]
Lieutenant.

Field command (V) 682, Namur 9.12.41
Command Section Ia 663/41

To: Military Commander in Belgium and Northern France
Command staff Ia

Brussels
Enclosure to daily report of 9.12.41
Re: Landing of enemy aircraft near Neufchateau [sic].

It was reported by Defence Section, Brussels, that on the night of
8 to 9 December an English aircraft would attempt to make a surprise
landing on the airstrip 3km north of Neufchateau [sic] to pick up a
Belgian Captain Cassard [sic]; the Regional Commander Neufchateau
was ordered to watch the airstrip unobtrusively and if possible to
capture the English aircraft, as well as arrest the persons involved.
As reinforcement of the forces of the Regional Commander were
made available: 1 platoon Fusiliers and the Military Police of Regional
Command Arlon and the MP of Regional Command Bastogne.
Additionally, the GFP Namur was directed to Neufchateau
immediately on receipt of the report.

The Regional Commander Neufchateau reports hereon:

On 8th December 1941 at 21.35 hours the Regional Command
Neufchateau 636 (3) was advised that during the period of 10.00 till
3.00am an English aircraft would land on the disused field airstrip
3km north of Neufchateau.

At 22.00 hours the Military Police Neufchateau in a strength of
1 officer and 18 men was mobilised. The strip was surrounded and
guarded (watched).

At 22.55 hours instructions came to search for Belgian cars Nos 888CD
and 443.

At 23.30 hours arrival of Military Police force Arlon in strength of 1
officer and 15 men and Bastogne in strength of 1 Staff Sergeant and 13
soldiers. The two groups were also detailed to guard and observe the
airstrip and made contact with Military Police force Neufchateau.

At 23.30 hours rifle fire was reported from the airstrip.

At 00.20 hours report from Military Police, Neufchateau, about the
finding of 2 suitcases and 2 Belgian officers' coats on the airstrip. At
the same time a report came that 2 civilians who wanted to approach
the suitcases were sighted, one of which [sic] was arrested but fled
again. A wallet with identity card and money as well as a pistol were
taken from the prisoner.

The arresting soldier demanded the prisoner to indicate the
location of the signal lights. At this occasion the prisoner managed
to escape. A shot fired at him missed owing to the darkness; the
subsequent jamming of the rifle assisted the flight.

The chase which began immediately did not lead to catching the
two escapees. At the same time, the finding of the signal lamps was
reported, and the order given to light the lamps in their positions –
triangle form, top red, base white. It comprised self-made battery
lamps with bicycle reflectors.

00.30 hours, arrival of Fusiliers Battalion 367 in strength of 1 officer
and 22 men. These were immediately employed in further searching
and isolation of greater area around airstrip.

00.45 hours, arrival of GFP 739 Namur under command of Field
Police Commissioner Wunson with 1 Sonderfuehrer, 1 Secretary and

6 men, who also entered the airstrip. Upon learning of the escape of both above mentioned, a detail of 1 NCO and 6 men was also employed within the town of Neufchateau. The guard in front of the 'Kommandantur' was reinforced to double sentries.

At 00.55 hours an enemy aircraft was noticed circling over Neufchateau and the airstrip. After concluding, because of the prolonged circling, that the aeroplane would not proceed to land, the substituted Area Commander requested through the Field Command, the employment of night fighters. In view of the importance of the functioning of the signalling lamps Captain Schnepp entered the airstrip to satisfy himself personally of this.

01.55 hours. The machine circling continuously at low altitude over the strip using a strong searchlight. Apparently the machine was looking for a suitable landing place. After one of the policemen gave white signal lights the machine commenced landing at 02.04 hours. The landing followed 300–400 metres from the red signal lamp in the direction of the top of the triangle. The MP forces of Neufchateau and Arlon approached the machine from two sides. One person alighted, apparently to orientate himself, but boarded immediately again.

When the most forward of the MPs had approached the machine to approx. 30 metres, the pilot accelerated – the machine was standing with running engines – and at the same moment all the rushing MPs opened fire.

Approximately 100 shots were fired and with certainty many hits were scored. In spite of this the machine managed to start and to disappear in eastern direction.

At 02.10 hours 3 officers of the Counter Espionage – Captain Brau, Captain Mohring and Captain Meurers – travelling from Brussels, arrived at the District Command.

The suitcases that were found, containing valuable material as well as the identity papers and the weapon taken from the prisoner were handed over to the Counter Espionage.

At the same time the GFP patrols from Namur were employed in

the triangle Neufchateau Road–Libramout–Neufchateau. The
Fusiliers from Arlon searched the area to the right of the road
Neufchateau–Libramout until La Mouline, also without results.
The 'Feldgendarmerie' of Arlon extended its patrol in the direction of
Bertrix until Petitvoir, while the 'Feldgendarmerie' went through the
town of Neufchateau and the village of Longlier. Also here nothing
could be ascertained.

The first trains in direction Libramout and Arlon were searched
for suspicious persons by the Feldgendarmerie Neufchateau without
results.

The units returning after daybreak have instructions to watch
sharply for suspicious persons, as well as for the two Belgian cars
during their return to their stations, and to make necessary arrests.
The Feldgendarmerie is presently searching the airstrip for items
dropped or left behind by the enemy.

This afternoon at 12 o'clock the Regional Command Neufchateau
reports that the Car registration number 888CD was found empty and
without passengers on the road Sehel–Tournay near Neufchateau.

On information from the Counter Espionage Brussels that the two
agents fired at during the past night at the airstrip were still near the
airstrip in a farmstead and that a short-wave transmitter must be
installed there; the investigations are continued by the Regional
Command.

The Field Commander
Signed: von Walther
Colonel
pp [illegible]
Captain.

Wing Commander Nesbitt-Dufort on his rescue by Sticky Murphy in an Anson, with others, and Sticky's report on the same trip

Extract from the Operations Record Book of No. 161 (Special Duty) Squadron:

Place: Operation 'Beryl II'
Date: 28.1.42
Summary of Events: Pilot S/Ldr J. Nesbitt-Dufort, DSO, a/c Lysander No. T.1508.

This hazardous operation was carried out while the pilot was a member of 138 Squadron, but in view of the denouement it must find a place in the annals of the squadron.

Hereunder follows a copy of the pilot's report:

1. Airborne 19.15hrs, approx., set course for Tronville. Called up regional control and received them strength 6, with slight whistle. Intercom working satisfactorily. Climbed to 9,000ft through thin cloud, experienced slight icing. The French coast was not observed but was able to pinpoint myself well to left of track, south of the Seine. Made alteration of course, and flying just below a thin layer of cloud pinpointed myself again on the Loire. Told passenger to prepare to disembark and map read to the target, reaching it at approx. 22.05hrs. Satisfactory landing made. Passenger and luggage disembarked, and two passengers and luggage embarked.

2. Take-off satisfactory, course set for home via Fecamp and Beachy Head; it was now raining quite hard and after talking to passengers for about ten minutes, the intercom failed, and as I could get no side-tone from my own mike, I rightly assumed that my radio had packed up completely. The weather deteriorated rapidly after first hour's flying, cloud being 10/10 at about 700ft and I was reduced to hedge-hopping in heavy rain and extremely bumpy conditions (typical line-squall).

3. A thin coat of glazed frost started to form on my windscreen and leading edge, so I decided to turn back and try again, after climbing above the bad weather, which had all the symptoms of a well-defined Cold Front. I was not very keen on doing this as I had not been able to make an accurate pinpoint before losing sight of the ground, owing to low cloud and rain and had not the facilities of my radio for homing over the Channel. I started to climb on my course from a D/R position of about 50 miles due south of the Seine (between Abbeville and the first loop) – course being set for Beachy Head.

4. I was now flying in very thick and bumpy cloud continuously. At first there was a slight misting of the windscreen, but at 7,000ft it started to rain and severe icing began at 8,000ft. The engine gave indications of ice in the air intake, and there was three or four inches of clear ice on the leading edge of the slots. I pulled the override in the hope that I might be able to clear, but at about 8,500ft I was gaining no height, and the aircraft was practically unmanageable (it must be remembered that there were two passengers and luggage in the back).

5. I estimated position was between the Seine and the French coast, so throttled back my engine and shouted to my passengers to bale out! They obviously could not hear me, as they did not do so. The aircraft would not now maintain height at full throttle, so I let the nose drop and tried to work her round on to a reciprocal course. Speed about 240mph by the time the aircraft had turned 180° and at 2,500ft I started to ease the aircraft out of the dive and broke cloud at about 1,000ft. On straightening out I found that in spite of a certain amount of ice that still adhered, the aircraft could still be flown straight and level

without much difficulty at a speed greater than 150mph. I flew west for about 40 miles, and then east for about 70 miles with the hope of finding a break in the Front. I had no success.

6. I had now been flying for over five and a half hours, most of which had been at high boost for climbing. I had now only 40 gallons of petrol in my main tank, and about 10 gallons in the auxiliary. Having satisfied myself it was impossible to get through the Front, I decided in view of the nature of my passengers and their luggage, it would be best to fly back to unoccupied France and 'force land' in the vicinity of Chateauroux [sic].

7. Setting a new course from my D/R position I recrossed the Loire at Orleans [sic], altered course for Issoudun, recrossing the demarcation line at Bourges knowing that it would not be healthy to land again at Issoudun aerodrome. I force-landed in the most likely looking field which unfortunately had a ditch running across the far end, which could not be seen in the dark. This resulted in the aircraft breaking the undercarriage, and turning up on its nose. No one was hurt, my passengers jumped out, and I tried to extract the axes, which had, however, got firmly wedged in the cockpit. A Jack Knife was used to tackle the bottom of the auxiliary petrol tank, which being self-sealing gave some difficulty. Eventually I managed to get petrol flowing and having exploded the IFF I fired one Very cartridge to set the aircraft on fire. Owing to shortage of petrol, I had some difficulty in getting the aircraft to burn. After two more cartridges, however, it seemed to be well alight, and we all ran for it, as we were only about 75 yards from a house. I am afraid that when we were about 2 kilometres away the fire must have gone out as we could see no glow coming from the direction of where we had left the aircraft.

8. Landed at 02.10hrs, having been in the air approx. 7 hours.

9. It has since been discovered that the aircraft had been totally destroyed by a locomotive at a level crossing while being towed away, and that a Curé has been arrested in Chateauroux under the impression

that he was the pilot of the aircraft!

The following is the narrative of Squadron Leader Dufort's enforced sojourn in foreign climes with his friends and the manner of his return home from the above operation. A truly interesting and exciting saga:

Having left the aircraft, two agents and myself being under the impression that we were a few miles to the left of Issoudun, proceeded to walk in an easterly direction. After three or four miles we came to St Florent from whence, by map, a roundabout route to Issoudun.

Walking another four miles, and having been flying continuously for 7 hours, I was too fatigued to proceed any further, and against the wishes of the two agents, decided to sleep in what hiding could be found near the road. One of the agents at considerable risk to himself insisted on staying with me, and we hid in a three-sided shepherd's hut about 100 yards from the road. It had been raining continually all night, a strong wind was blowing and it was very cold. The other agent proceeded on foot to Issoudun, arriving there about 7 o'clock in the morning where he managed with considerable difficulty to obtain a car with a driver. He picked us up at about 2pm the following day.

He had also managed to find somewhere for us to hide on the railway station at Issoudun, and arriving there we were given a hot meal and made most welcome. The agent who had stayed with me had a couple of hours sleep and proceeded south by train that evening to try to get news of our predicament through, with the least delay.

For the following 30 days I was forced to stay indoors, as I had no identity card or food tickets. I was very well looked after, and apart from lack of minor luxuries, such as cigarettes, reading material and exercise, I was extremely comfortable, if somewhat cold on occasions.

Two days before date of departure, one of the agents was able to finish forging an identity card for me, and the night before the operation I was taken for a walk through the town and shown the direction I was to take, to and from the aerodrome, should we get separated.

On the night of departure, the BBC signal came through very indistinctly through jamming, but a few words were just audible. This was at 6.15 and at 7 o'clock the fourth member of the party arrived from the south where he had been delayed due to illness, and at 7.45, having had a square meal, the four of us set out with a minimum of luggage, which consisted of one rather heavy suitcase, carried in turn by the four of us to Issoudun. We made very good time and arrived at the aerodrome at 9.30, rested for 15 minutes and then proceeded to lay the flarepath out, the dimensions of which I propose to adopt as standard for this type of work in future.

By 10 o'clock we were all in position lying on the ground. We were not bothered by anyone in any way, but barking of dogs gave the impression that they were uncomfortably close. We had two false alarms, and on each occasion the flarepath was lit, and I signalled frantically to what later on turned out to be friendly Whitleys. They did not see me, however.

At midnight our ETA was up and one of the agents approached me on the subject of waiting any longer and we decided that it was possible that we had made some mistake over the time, and we should wait until 1 o'clock. At 12.15 the unmistakeable noise of an Anson approaching at low altitude and high speed was heard from the north. The flarepath was lit and signals sent and answered promptly. The aircraft did one circuit and made a beautiful landing without wasting unnecessary time. It was then signalled to the edge of the aerodrome and embarkation was carried out without a hitch at high speed. After a hasty conference with the pilot on the advisability of one member of the crew getting out again and pushing, to assist the take-off, we decided against this somewhat drastic course, and after 8 or 9 anxious minutes 'Gormless Gertie', the aircraft in question, achieved a speed corresponding to a smart trot, having passed No. 2 and No. 3 lights earlier in the evening. On proceeding at a slightly increased but rather dangerous speed, we found to our amazement that we were airborne.

The pilot informed me that if it had not been for the almost previously unheard of and drastic use of 'skyhooks' this undoubtedly would not have been accomplished.

The remainder of the trip to base was uneventful if slow. The skill of the pilot and navigator proved in this case to be exceptional, as we were only lost the majority of the way home.

The following narrative by the pilot describes his side of the 'finis' to the above 'Continental holiday':

Place: Operations 'Beryl II and III'
Date: 1/2 March
Time: 21.00
Summary of Events: Anson 'R' 3316 – S/Ldr A.M. Murphy, DFC; P/O Cossar, Wireless Operator

We became airborne at Tangmere at 21.00hrs, set course for Cabourg, reached at 22.00 a height of 9,000ft. Course then set for Tours. Visibility remained excellent until a point was reached 40 miles north of Tours, when 10/10 cloud encountered with heavy precipitation, visibility in nature of 1,000 yards. Some time was spent in pinpointing the Loire and eventually course was set for Chateauroux [sic] at 23.15hrs.

Visibility remained poor and I lost myself at 23.30hrs, but eventually reached Chateauroux at 23.55hrs. Course set for Issoudun and lights picked up at 00.10hrs.

Landing completed without trouble, and the four passengers embarked very rapidly. We then became airborne again at 00.15hrs and set course for Cabourg.

We pinpointed ourselves over the Loire and the Seine and crossed the French coast at Dieppe at 22.00hrs. Course was set for base and we landed at 02.40hrs.

(The unofficial note in the Operations Record Book of No. 161 Squadron is in Chapter 5.)

Harry Cossar's report on the Anson trip

The following is the account of Pilot Officer Harry Cossar, DFC, regarding the Anson pick-up on 1 March 1942:

I flew on fifty operations in all as a wireless operator/air gunner, but this particular one stands out most in my memory.

I flew on operations with thirteen different skippers but only two remain clearly recalled. Sticky was one of these two, and I can well imagine his influence as a squadron commander. I would have followed him to Hell and back.

In July 1941 I completed a tour of thirty bomber operations on Blenheims, Wellingtons and Stirlings and was posted to Newmarket for a rest period and to run a refresher course for wireless operators from squadrons within No. 3 Bomber Group where I had managed to remain.

My impression of Newmarket in the ensuing months was that of a small reasonably healthy training unit but with a few 'elusive bods' coming and going and with Lysanders and Whitleys. People continually evaded questions as to what they were used for, but slowly I gleaned the significance of what was going on, but was still very much in the dark and stopped asking questions.

By this time the officers' mess was at Sefton Lodge, one of the famous horseracing trainer's establishments. I had become friendly with two chaps in the mess who were Johnny Dufort and Sticky Murphy. It was all one happy family but with very different pursuits.

I recall Sticky as a very friendly, pleasant chap, always laughing and joking, but I also recall that he had been shot through the neck on an operation, but had managed to bring his aircraft back, and I did not see him for some little time after that.

In about February 1942 I learned that Johnny Dufort was missing from one operation. In about the middle of that month I had a conversation with Sticky in the mess when he said, 'Tich, can I have a word with you?' I replied, 'Fire away old lad.' Sticky went on, 'I'm going to fetch Johnny Dufort. Will you come and help me; I can't give you any details except that it will be an Anson and we'll be landing in France.'

I tried to gather my composure, astounded at the calmness of the request, and then said, 'Alright Sticky, when do we go?'

He explained that he was borrowing an Anson, which would have to be fitted with an overload petrol tank, wireless gear and a gun. He asked if I would supervise the fitting of this equipment and I agreed but asked why he needed an Anson. Sticky replied, 'Well I'd rather have someone to guard my tail. If I get lost on the way back you can always get me a QDM.' This was a course to steer from base which I could obtain by wireless telegraphy.

The Anson duly arrived at Newmarket and was fitted out for the trip and we did night-flying take-off and landing tests, principally I think to see how quick an approach could be made and how short a landing distance he could achieve. I complied with the necessary speed in lowering the undercarriage and flaps and tested the wireless and guns. He seemed to be satisfied with the performance and a temporary transfer was arranged for me from my unit to 161 Squadron.

Finally we went down to Tangmere a few days before the operation and waited for favourable conditions and signals. We were billeted in a house just off the airfield and only went out under supervision in a chauffeur-driven Rolls-Royce car. Security was obviously very tight and during those two days or so there were two or three civilians, including a woman (whom I learned later were French agents either going to France or coming back).

At about noon on 1 March 1942, it was decided that weather conditions were probably as good as could be expected for that time of the year, and the trip was on. It was only after this time that I was told where we were going, and even then I was not shown the exact landing zone, only that we were making for Châteauroux. With this information I immediately went to the airfield to set up my wireless transmitter on the Tangmere Direction Finding frequency and did the necessary tests and made sure that everyone would keep their ears glued for my call- sign on the way back.

The take-off was uneventful and after winding up the undercarriage and we had been on course for a couple of minutes or so, Sticky motioned me back to the gun turret, which is not the easiest place to get into, even for a small man, loaded up with night-flying clobber. After pushing down the spring-loaded seat I settled down and reached for the intercom socket and couldn't find it, and therefore got out of my turret and groped around and found it smashed to smithereens in the angle of the turret seat. It was impossible to make a repair without being out of the turret for a considerable length of time and I went up front and reported to Sticky, who considered the situation, and we then arranged that he would waggle his wings if he wanted me to come up front, and I should fire a couple of short bursts if there was danger about.

His calmness settled my doubts and I went back to the turret, cocked the Vickers gas-operated machine gun and swung the turret to make sure nothing was fouling it, and then tried to relax for the long silent vigil.

I could not see much over the Channel and it seemed to be a long time before we reached the French coast, and there was no light or sign of life as far as I could see.

Horror of horrors, when we got over the land everything seemed to light up! There was snow on the ground and I could see for miles. We must have been beautifully silhouetted for anything above, and an absolutely sitting duck at our speed of 100 knots. My concentration settled in an arc above us with just the necessary scanning below, but there was nothing for mile after mile. At one time I detected a silhouette just below but out of range. I concentrated for a long time but nothing materialised.

After what seemed to be an interminable length of time, I felt the

wings waggle, got out of the turret and went up the front and Sticky
said, 'We're just coming up to the Loire, Tich; I'm going down to see
if I can get a good pinpoint.'

We came down to about 1,000 feet and flew along the river for quite
a distance before Sticky was satisfied and then he set course south
again. He did not attempt to gain much height and after about twenty
minutes we were over a town and he changed course to port, very
shortly, saying, 'Right Tich, look out for the signal', and he proceeded
to do a couple of circuits but there was nothing.

After commenting that we were running short of petrol, he set
course back to the town we had just left, which I now realise was
probably Châtillon. Then realising that he had been off course a little
from the Loire, he altered course again and said, 'We've only got about
fifteen or twenty minutes more Tich.'

Almost immediately I could see faint lights ahead and said, 'Could
that be Châteauroux, Sticky?' Actually I thought my eyes were playing
tricks when I saw what I thought were lights, but sure enough as we
approached I could see the streets quite plainly with the masked street
lamps shining down on the pavements.

He immediately changed course and my eyes strained through the
darkness as we went on and on and suddenly there was a pinpoint of
light flashing: . − . . − ., the [Morse code for the] letter 'R'. I directed his
gaze slightly to starboard and as he saw the signal he almost shouted,
'Undercart.' I wound furiously as he banked round and then almost
immediately, 'Flaps.' I had hardly finished when we were over the
hedge and on the ground.

Sticky wheeled the Anson round before it came to a standstill and
taxied back. 'Open the door, Tich,' he shouted as the Anson was
wheeling round again and came to a standstill as I opened the door.
Four dark figures came round the tail one after the other, the leading
figure pointing an automatic pistol straight at my chest. I hesitated …
'Is that you Johnny?' The automatic dropped. I grasped the out-
stretched hand and directed the uplifted foot into the teo recess, calling
each one aboard in the same manner and directing them forward.
I closed the door and gave the 'Go' on the intercom, then climbed
into the turret as the Anson moved forward.

A little prayer, and the engines roared, then we just cleared the hedge and were on our way back. Again the constant scanning for any enemy aircraft, but now a little more relaxed. Sticky seemed to be gaining height very slowly.

I had not realised up to this time how cold I was, and reached for the flask of coffee. Someone had laced it with whisky, and I must say the result was very encouraging. As time went on I mused to myself that they must have thought it was one of their own communication aircraft chugging along, but nevertheless I still kept a constant watch.

A tug at the back of my left leg, and a note thrust around my shoulder from Sticky for a QDM (course to steer) for Tangmere. I quickly got this and passed it to Sticky.

I think we must have been just crossing the French coast at this time, as it seemed to be a long time afterwards that Sticky told us that he would be making a steep approach in case the engines cut out on the way for lack of petrol. He banked and the nose came down and we were on the runway before we knew what had happened, and with the help of a little prayer.

When we left the aircraft there was a welcoming party of several people, including Wing Commander 'Mouse' Fielden. We were whisked immediately back to the house where meat and drink was already laid out for us, and the celebration began.

Needless to say, by the time I got out of bed Johnny Dufort had left for London to be reunited with his wife, and Sticky was in no mood to be approached by anybody. Strangely, I can't remember how or when I got back to Newmarket, but a little later on, when Johnny Dufort came back from leave, he and I and Sticky had a special celebration dinner in Newmarket.

Film Project

We are at Luqa Aerodrome, Malta, G.C. in September, 1943. Nearby are
battered iron huts and bomb shelters with aircraft parked. There is a
bright blue sky and a white runway. Four men stand in a group looking
upward. On close inspection we notice that they wear RAF battledress,
yellow Mae Wests and carry parachutes – two pilot and two observer
types. One man, short and stocky, wears an Australian bush hat. He is a
Sergeant Pilot of the Royal Australian Air Force named 'Shorty' Dawson.
Beside him is his observer, Sergeant Fergie Murray, aged 35, stocky,
greying and a Londoner. They are a Mosquito crew of No. 23 Intruder
Squadron, seconded from Fighter Command. The pilot of the other
crew is Sergeant Pilot Bill Shattock, 5'10', of medium muscular build
and steady gaze. With his large hands and Somerset speech he is a
farmer and looks it. He is aged 25 years. All four men are deeply sun-
burned, hungry and weary. His observer, Sergeant Jim Coley, 6' 4" and
less than 140 lbs in weight, is dark with a moustache and shows the lack
of food they have all suffered from in Malta. He is aged 22 years. They
have a short conversation about the Mosquito circling to land – bringing
reinforcements.

We cut to the aircraft which makes a perfect three-wheel landing and
taxies to a halt near the standing group. An erk takes the ladder offered
from inside the aircraft and a tall slim man emerges wearing RAF blue, a
Mae West, flying helmet and observer's parachute harness and carrying
a green navigation bag. He stands aside and the pilot comes out, wearing

a Mae West over a black one piece flying suit. He reaches the ground, takes off a flying helmet and shakes his head. A pale face lights up with a smile. He looks around in a friendly way. A tall athletic figure completes his appearance as he sweeps his full moustache upwards on both wings. Peeling off his Mae West and black suit reveals RAF wings, a squadron leader's rings on his shoulders and DSO, DFC, and Croix de Guerre ribbons. Shorty has a short conversation with him about an oil leak on the starboard engine and the whereabouts of 'the bog'. The newcomer's voice is pukka RAF but with a fresh and friendly tone. He looks very fit and pleased to be in Malta.

We hear Shorty and the others discuss the new arrivals whom they regard with some doubt. Shorty says 'A Pommy squadron leader named Stinky something or other.'

We see the two crews board their Mosquitoes and take off, forming close formation as they swoop over an elderly battered American car in which Sticky Murphy and the navigator Flight Lieutenant Bilbe-Robinson are driven to the Officers Mess, Meadowbank Hotel, Sliema, on the seafront. The two Mosquitoes skim the waves like speedboats.

In the bar we see Sticky quietly and modestly chatting to other officers when he is told that the two crews who met him have gone to Sicily to refuel and then bomb aerodromes near Rome. He asks very professional questions about flying and operating conditions from the Commanding Officer Wing Commander Peter Burton-Gyles, DSO, DFC, only to be told that he has just arrived himself and there are only six aircraft and eleven crews.

Peter Burton-Gyles is aged 25, a shy, dark-haired veteran airman of medium height and build. Squadron Leader Sticky Murphy is 26 two days after his arrival. His effervescent personality and natural leadership contrast with the new CO although they get on well together.

We see Sticky Murphy fly in very close formation with Bill Shattock and Squadron Leader Paul Rabone, whom he is replacing. They gambol around the leader, Shattock, exchanging positions, not far above the mountainous terrain, en route to the landing ground on the Catanian plain. In Sicily in a tent the CO and Squadron Leader Murphy consume numerous fried eggs with their fingers.

Now we cut back to 1917 to the Lake District and see Cockermouth and Murphy's birthplace, a modest home of his father George, mother Ethel and sister Doreen, three years old when Sticky is born.

Then we see Canford School near Wimborne, Dorset on a sports day where a teenage Alan Murphy runs in the 440 yards, then 110 yards hurdles and the high jump and long jump. His family are there. Alan is popular and bubbling with life and enthusiasm. We pan round the grounds, chapel and school, and to the nearby Murphy home, 'Morland', Ferndown, for a moment. It is 1935.

Next we see RAF College, Cranwell on a sports day as the now Flight Cadet Sticky Murphy breaks the RAF long jump record with 23'1 ¾". It is 1937.

Suddenly the mood changes at Cranwell. We see aircraft manned ready for take-off but stationary, and then a German Mercedes car appears and Ernst Udet, Milch and Stumpff get out in uniform and exchange salutes with due ceremony. A green Very light is fired almost immediately, and aircraft take off like a covey of partridges in all directions. The German Luftwaffe Generals' remarks are overheard.

The young Flight Cadet Murphy is seen with his instructor and solo, having emergencies, propeller stopping during aerobatics, showing courage and sangfroid! Also, we see him off duty, swimming and drinking with good friends racing in old sports cars, and hill climbing.

Then comes the passing out 'Wings' parade where Murphy is one of three Under-Officers on parade.

We see now the headlines of Germany's breakthrough at Sedan and in a

Wellington bomber find Flying Officer Murphy in the second pilot's seat as bridges over the River Somme are bombed on the 10 June,1940. From the conversation on the way back we realise that Murphy has no business to be there but has forced his way into action en route to Lossiemouth as a Navigation Instructor.

There we see his short courtship with his wife Jean Leggat, a tiny 20 year old newly commissioned Assistant Section Officer of the WAAF and their marriage when he is serving on No. 1419 Special Duty Flight at Newmarket. There is a hectic good natured party on the wedding evening at Hatchetts in the West End, and a wasp crawls up the leg of the bride in the church at Newbury as the couple are kneeling before the priest. Sticky is in the uniform of a flight lieutenant and Jean wears high heels and silk stockings and is wearing a dress.

We see them at their honeymoon hotel at Broadway (The Lygon Arms) and the repeated telephoning throughout the night by fellow officers insisting that they have urgent messages for him.

We see him in a different guise as a complete professional pilot dropping Agents from Whitleys at night and taking a 'boffin' in a white overall on special experiments with an 'S' phone which has been invented for contact between agents on the ground and airmen above. We see flak and searchlights around the Whitley. John Nesbitt-Dufort, the first successful Lysander pilot is the co-pilot with Sticky Murphy. The 'boffin' is Charles Bovill who finds their reassuring comments about the lights and explosions around them very touching. They do not realise he is a veteran airman who has worked for Marconi for many years past.

Also we see an incident where Sticky takes the body of an Agent wrapped up in a shroud and weighted and drops it over the English Channel as the man had been strangled by his own parachute shrouds the night before on an abortive dropping exercise.

We then switch to Tangmere Aerodrome on 8 December 1941, where John Nesbitt-Dufort has a streaming cold and they are laughing, with two black Lysanders with steps attached to them and torpedo-like extra petrol tanks slung beneath. We then hear the medical officer tell John that he cannot fly under any circumstances. Sticky interrupts to say that his flight that night has been cancelled. He wishes to take John's place. Lord Philip Rea, the SOE Officer there to collect and interrogate the returning Agent asks that some attempt be made to rescue the Agent who is in danger from the Gestapo. We then see Sticky check weather forecasts and all other information and obtain the most secret initial 'L' from John Nesbitt-Dufort which is the one agreed only between that person and the Agent (coming from the Belgian Agent), the initial of his sovereign Leopold.

Then we see Sticky whistling to himself in the aircraft as he flies across the snow-covered Continent on the long run down to Neufchâteau in the Ardennes where he is due late that night.

We switch to conditions in the moonlight on the snow-covered fields surrounding Neufchâteau near a wood. Three men get out of a car dressed in civilian clothes and quietly walk through to a field with lamps in their hands to set the primitive flarepath for the expected aircraft. The leader of the men is slim and about 5' 9" tall and is a captain of the Belgian Army named Jean Cassart. He has two suitcases. As they come through the trees on the edge of a disused airfield they see other persons moving and hear a challenge in German. Dropping the suitcases, as a number of shots ring out, Captain Cassart throws himself to his right and runs despite being shot in the left arm. He keeps going through a ditch, a stream and barbed wire until completely exhausted he collapses in the snow beneath the wall of Neufchâteau Cemetery.

We see the other man taken prisoner by the Germans and threatened with pistols at his head and the third man disappears into the night.

Shortly afterwards we hear the sound of the approaching Lysander. As the Germans search for Captain Cassart, the other prisoner makes his escape and there are numerous bright torches flashing in the woods and surrounding district by many soldiers. Shouts of command resound.

We switch to Sticky now in the Lysander. He sees lights far exceeding those he expects to see at this particular field. He decides that the Agent is in great danger and after flying round, he lands, having hurdled a ditch where the Germans have set out landing lamps. At the end of the snow-covered field he turns ready to receive his passengers with a revolver cocked. He sees flashing lights coming towards him and thinks that they are Belgian Agents. Suddenly he realises that they are machine guns firing at him and takes off immediately, feeling a blow in the neck. The bullet goes through the front of his neck and out at the back, and the aircraft is badly damaged by gunfire.

We see him nurse the aircraft back to the Belgian coast across to Kent and along the coast towards Tangmere where John Nesbitt-Dufort is now seen at the Controller's desk full of anxiety because Sticky is over-due. Eventually a short whisper comes through on the radio and Nesbitt-Dufort takes over the microphone and in the appropriate code asks Sticky about the way his mission has gone. Sticky said that the 'oranges are bloody bitter' which means some disaster has taken place. This is obvious by the ground speed of his aircraft which is much less than usual. With appropriate lies as to the time and distance needed, Nesbitt-Dufort nurses Sticky on the appropriate course, by radio, back to base. He lands and gets out of the aircraft. His reception committee see that down his left side is a mess as if a large saucepan of melted chocolate has been poured over him. His remark on landing is, 'whoopee John, I've been wounded! Please get a wound stripe for me from Gieves!'.

At Chichester Hospital the following morning we see Sticky's wife in WAAF uniform by his bedside. Sticky has a bottle of whisky hidden under the bedclothes and a glass. John joins them and has a glass of whisky, Sticky complaining , 'I told them when they gave me a blood transfusion that they might be interfering with the delicate balance of my blood-alcohol level!'. At this moment Matron comes in, finding John Nesbitt with bottle and glass in his hand. Sticky's glass has disappeared under the bedclothes, but his boyish grin remains. Matron says, 'I hope you are not encouraging this patient to drink. We are having enough difficulty with him already.'

Next we see Sticky with the DFC ribbon on his chest from this exploit and it is conveyed to him by an Intelligence Officer that the Belgian Resistance have sent a message to the effect, 'Congratulations to the pilot for landing despite no signal to do so, and hope he was not wounded.'

Now in the Officers' Mess at Newmarket, Sticky Murphy has a conversation with wireless operator/air gunner Pilot Officer Harry 'Tich' Cossar asking him quietly to come on a special mission in an Anson aircraft deep into France to rescue John Nesbitt-Dufort and other persons. It is February, 1942.

Now we are in the Anson Aircraft at night looking down on a moonlit Europe with rivers and fields and no conversation possible between the pilot and rear gunner (wireless operator) who are respectively Sticky Murphy and Tich Cossar. Their intercom is not working. By signals at the last moment we see Cossar indicating a field and a flashing light. A hurried landing is made and John Nesbitt-Dufort puts a gun in the face of Cossar when checking identification, before loading two French Agents with himself and a stocky grey-haired Polish General. John greets Sticky with the words 'You old bastard.' Sticky replies, 'You stink like a Paris Metro!'.

We hear a short conversation about being lost before they land at Tangmere when we see a big party with food and drink take place immediately, celebrating the return of Nesbitt-Dufort after five weeks in enemy territory. One of the persons greeting Sticky and John is the Commanding Officer of No. 161 Squadron Wing Commander 'Mouse' Fielden, MVC, H.M. George VI's personal pilot and Commander of the King's Flight. Later we see Wing Commander Fielden telling Sticky Murphy that he has been awarded the DSO for his last flight and others and that he will be rested shortly at the Air Ministry. Sticky takes both announcements quietly but writes in a private log book, 'THIS WAS THE GREATEST FUN EVER.'

Now we see Sticky with a cannon, firing paper projectiles across Kingsway towards the offices on the other side, saying in a telephone conversation, 'I'm just cheesed off. I manage to fly a few types but admin is not for me.'

Now we see Sticky Murphy at High Ercall in sight of the 'Wrekin' in Shropshire at No. 60 OTU where he is about to fly with Squadron Leader Phil Russell DFC in the Mosquito Mark VI aircraft where he is to train for intruders and to go to No. 23 Squadron in Malta as a reinforcement. It is June 1943.

We see shots of him in the Mosquito and carrying out a solo landing and then flying with his navigator Flying Officer Jock Reid (a dour Scot) in training exercises. Then we see them on transit to Malta at Lyneham where Sticky tells Jock late at night as they lie in their bunks, that he would have liked to have been alive in the age of chivalry where each man relied on his speed, skill and strength in personal combat.

Again, as at the beginning, we see Sticky with another navigator landing in Malta.

Then we see Sticky bringing four bottles of wine into a room sparsely furnished in Malta occupied by the four people who met him on his arrival in Malta, plus John Irvin and his pilot George Twitt. He says 'I have been looking at the papers. You chaps have been holding the fort. What is the gen? Let's have a drink.'

We see Jim Coley and Shorty Dawson exchange looks behind his back and gently shake their heads and a conversation takes place during which all gently question Sticky about his flying experience. He is vague about his operational career, so that they drink his wine and tell him such vague things as, 'The compasses are dodgy out here with the volcanic terraine,' and 'You always overshoot Malta when coming back from the heel of Italy,' and 'On dark nights over Sicily you have to watch out for 10,750 ft high Mount Etna. Use the volcanoes Stromboli and Vesuvius as navigational aids, because the Met forecasts are always wrong out here and we have to bring them back for the day fighters and bombers.' Sticky departs from the room and afterwards Shorty says,

'Seems a decent sort of a bloke for a Pom, I wonder what he has been up to. He did not get those gongs for sitting around boozing and talking.'

Now we are on the bare airfield of Luqa as six crews are about to leave Malta and pose for a photograph (which exists) behind Maltese girls selling red poppies for Armistice Day. It is the 11 November 1943.

Then we see the aircraft approaching, in bright blue sky, the vicinity of the Isle of Capri and the Bay of Naples, as they individually land at Pomigliano on the Plain of Naples, where they are later seen in wellington boots amongst snow and mud in tents, celebrating, with drinks, a hard-hitting night against the German reinforcement transport system to the Front. This is about thirty miles north of the aerodrome where No. 23 Squadron 'B' Flight are now operating and where Sticky Murphy is the Flight Commander. Wing Commander Burton-Gyles is also there and he and Sticky are still eating fried eggs in large quantities with their fingers.

Next morning we see a swooping cloud of low level FW190's dropping bombs and firing cannon and machine gun as they swoop across the section of the aerodrome (which is packed with American Aircraft) occupied by No. 23 Squadron. We see various members of the Squadron throwing themselves into slit trenches beside their tents as this is a dawn raid in riposte for the many attacks made by No. 23 Squadron Mosquitoes on the two preceding nights. One squadron member has nearly strangled himself with a lanyard attached to his revolver and has split his trousers and moans, 'Look at the damage they have done to me', which causes the others to burst into laughter as much in thanks for no real damage being done as in recognition of his plight.

Now we are at barrack blocks in Sardinia for the Christmas party of No. 23 Squadron when Sticky has become Commanding Officer after the loss of Wing Commander Burton-Gyles in the days just before Christmas 1943, and where a substantial booze up takes place with ample food including pigs which have been bought locally (the menu remains available).

Following Christmas at Alghero Aerodrome with 'Murphy's Mountain',
a 1400' hill on the circuit where night approaches in the pitch black at
500ft are common, we see a night flying test of aircraft in progress.
Viewing from a cluster of airmen, not due to fly that night, on the
control tower, we see an aircraft stutter on take-off and then plough in
with a high funeral pyre of black smoke. We hear Sticky Murphy shout,
'Everybody airborne at once. Quick chaps! Low flying practice!' as he
runs for the jeep bearing the name 'De Doity Twenty Toid' accompanied
by Flight Lieutenant Buddy Badley and the squadron doctor. Then we
see them standing in swampland watching impotently the crew roast
to death in the burning Mosquito as other aircraft rise through the
black smoke into the sky and circle in pairs as they fly low over the
surrounding area in practice for Daylight RANGERS to come.

That night we see a typical No. 23 Squadron party in progress, which is
quite modest and restrained until Sticky Murphy lets fly with 'RIP MY
KNICKERS AWAY' in a style robust but raucous. Then the Mess, for
all flying personnel and NCO's and officers, erupts into 'We're a shower
of bastards', the squadron song, followed by 'Jesus wants me for a
sunbeam', 'I lefty my girl quite early', 'The Hamburg Zoo' and numerous
other traditional ditties. As time wears on the number is reinforced by
crews from dusk patrols who join in and furiously drink up to catch up
with the well-oiled state of their fellows. We watch one such crew land
in the dark, with poor visibility, see them debriefed and hurry to drink
before food, well twitched. We see others with various stages of the
twitch, including one with an imaginary dog and another promising
his male organ great delights the next day at the local brothel, where
we see a queue formed and guarded by airmen to keep the line orderly.

We notice two women in scanty dresses coming out of the house taking
dog ends from behind their ears and lighting them, having a few puffs
and stubbing them out and returning 'to duty' inside the house.

We see the party end with Sticky leading a charge in his jeep to the
brothel at 2.00 a.m. where banging on the stout doors produces only
abuse from within and they retreat in the rain singing as they go the

same songs over again.

Suddenly we switch to Algiers where a Command Ball is in progress and Sticky is in best uniform drinking excitedly with the AOC Air Vice Marshal Sir Hugh Pughe Lloyd and other senior officers, and inviting the AOC to visit the best squadron under his command.

Whilst Sticky is living it up in Algiers, we see three crashes on a filthy night when Pat Rapson and Frank White, Kit Cotter and Al Yates and finally Bill Shattock and Jim Coley scatter Mosquitoes across the runway for a variety of reasons, the latter crew having flown at about 600 ft in strong winds from Marseilles to Sardinia, so that they could hardly see out of their windscreen to land by the two or three gooseneck oil flares, which was all the illumination available because of the change of runway, because of the crashes of the two previous crews. They fly straight into the ground with a bang and a bounce.

The next day we see Sticky Murphy mention to one of his crews that he had flown back with Group Captain MacDonald and it was clear and bright outside but rather foggy inside the cockpit.

We hear talk of the impending invasion of Europe from England and the suggestion that the Squadron will be returning shortly to England.

Then we are in a big hall at a party thrown by the Americans where there are numerous women and their keepers and a massive punch bowl is filled with all types of spirit to which is added pure medicinal alcohol. We see a blonde Sophie Loren type of woman swagger up to the punch bowl and drink half a pint as if it was water whilst there is dancing going on in a rather desultory fashion, the 'keepers' keeping a close eye on the stairs which lead to the bedrooms. Music comes from a wind-up gramophone. We see the same magnificent blonde drink another half pint of the concoction and then do a slow strip dance until she is completely nude at which point she suddenly passes out like a light and is hurriedly carried to a place of rest by eager hands, despite the protests of her 'escort'.

We then see a member of the squadron going round borrowing money from the others as he 'wants to buy that beauty for life'. We see other dancing to a gramophone, and general skylarking, and suddenly we see the blonde, now dressed and wide awake, slung across the shoulder of the eager airman of No. 23 Squadron, Sabine style, as he makes for the stairs leading to the bedrooms only to be intercepted by several brother officers who unload him of his burden and also persuade him in to a side room to hand back their money which he had borrowed. The party ends with the squadron song sung at the top of their voices and much shaking of hands with the Americans. Sticky is noticeable in his exuberant style. As Jock Reid staggers out he is covered with tomato sauce on his best uniform and Bill Gregory faints in the truck he is waiting to drive.

Now we are in a shed beside Liverpool Docks where Sticky in smartest uniform greets his crews who have just arrived on a troop ship, the CO having flown home earlier in the month of May 1944. He announces that he is the father of a daughter and that the squadron is moving to Little Snoring which produces hoots and shouts of congratulations and good humour as they all make for the nearest public house to celebrate both lots of news in traditional fashion.

We then see Little Snoring airfield from the air on a broad flat expanse near Fakenham, Norfolk, and where there is already one squadron No. 515, commanded by Wing Commander Lambert, of Mosquitoes and we hear the briefing by Sticky of his crew to the effect that No. 23 is now a Bomber Support squadron of No. 100 Group of Bomber Command, and their function is to destroy the German night flying capacity which has caused such havoc amongst Bomber Command.

Sticky points out that it is a great honour to lead this effort and that there will be other daylight efforts and a variety of tasks now falling to No. 23 Squadron as the elite intruder squadron. Also we see Group Captain Sammy Hoare, DSO, DFC, who is station commander and still flies on operations and is known as the 'Intruder King', and we see Sticky holding his patience as Group Captain Hoare seems to regard his old squadron where he was commander for a long time, as his personal property, but they share a hut and seem to be on the best of terms. At the same time Group Captain Hoare is a very stern disciplinarian and does not approve of Sticky's methods of popping thunderflashes down hut chimneys, shouting a warning and sometimes not putting one down. At the same time we see Sticky at the other end of such a jape when he is taking a disciplinary hearing and has to flee the room with the Defendant and escort, as somebody has popped one into his office chimney and the soot has flown everywhere. He merely resumes the hearing and dismisses the charge.

We now see him showing some signs of stress and strain as he is approaching ninety operations and Flight Lieutenant Jock Reid, his navigator, who has his wife living near the airfield with him, complains that there is too big a space between the operations as Sticky is trying to string out his time and not return to any sort of staff duty or staff college, which is his immediate likely fate.

We see a melange of aircraft taking off, dropping bombs, strafing and similar efforts and then we are in a farmhouse adjacent to the aerodrome with a Mrs Bessie Whitehead in her fifties, acting as mother to the overseas crews, particularly, and with Sticky as her favourite. We see her cooking him Norfolk cakes with ingredients he has smuggled from the cookhouse and Sticky eating them hot in the kitchen, calling her 'Bess' and loving the home atmosphere that was there. We see him sitting with his boots off with other members around a roaring fire in the early hours, happily inebriated and when someone walks into the farmhouse door, Sticky call out, 'Come in old boy. I don't know who you are, but you are very welcome to join the party!' This turns out to be Mr Whitehead who likes a drink himself and with whom Sticky becomes on great terms.

We see Sticky in civilian clothes and wearing American paratrooper's jump boots, mixing with the local civilian population and shooting in the woodlands in the vicinity. We also see him reading the lesson at Little Snoring Church which is situated on the airfield, at a church parade. We see him in a telephone box on 2 December 1944 calling his wife and saying, 'A Wing Commander's moon tonight darling. Just one more trip.' We then see him leaving the telephone kiosk and bumping into Jock Reid who has just come from the medical quarters and has been grounded because of inflammation in the ears following very cold nights, and when Jock tells him this Sticky says that he will be flying with someone else that night. We see a Flight Sergeant Darbon, a stocky, fair haired young man, getting into the Mosquito after Sticky, and we follow them in a conversation in the air as they attack the German nightfighter Headquarters base at Gütersloh following heavy radar jamming in the whole area. We then see them hitting the top of trees just before they reach the safety of the Zuider Zee so that they plunge into the ground with a huge explosion.

We see the squadron next morning with the shock and disbelief that Sticky has been lost and that night we see a huge party in No. 23 Squadron tradition which is in no way a wake but a celebration of the great qualities of the man who had disappeared.

Index